MINOR PROPHETS II

Nahum, Habakkuk, Zephaniah, Haggai, Zechariah, Malachi

MINOR PROPHETS II

Nahum, Habakkuk, Zephaniah, Haggai, Zechariah, Malachi

GRACE EMMERSON

DOUBLEDAY BIBLE COMMENTARY
DOUBLEDAY
NEW YORK • LONDON • TORONTO • SYDNEY • AUCKLAND

DOUBLEDAY BIBLE COMMENTARY
PUBLISHED BY DOUBLEDAY
a division of Bantam Doubleday Dell Publishing Group, Inc.
1540 Broadway, New York, New York 10036

DBC, DOUBLEDAY, and the portrayal of an anchor with a dolphin are trademarks of
Doubleday, a division of Bantam Doubleday Dell Publishing Group, Inc.

Library of Congress Cataloging-in-Publication Data
Emmerson, Grace.
Minor prophets II: Nahum, Habakkuk, Zephaniah, Haggai, Zechariah, Malachi /
Grace Emmerson. — 1st ed. in the U.S.
p.   cm. — (Doubleday Bible commentary)
Includes bibliographical references.
1. Bible. O.T. Minor Prophets—Commentaries. 2. Bible. O.T. Minor Prophets—Devotional
literature. I. Title. II. Series.
BS1560.E55   1998
224′.907—dc21   98-22985
CIP

ISBN 0-385-49018-6

1 3 5 7 9 10 8 6 4 2

First Edition in the United States of America

Doubleday
Bible Commentary
Series

Congratulations! You are embarking on a voyage of discovery—or rediscovery. You may feel you know the Bible very well; you may never have turned its pages before. You may be looking for a fresh way of approaching daily Bible study; you may be searching for useful insights to share in a study group or from a pulpit.

The Doubleday Bible Commentary (DBC) series is designed for all those who want to study the scriptures in a way that will warm the heart as well as instruct the mind. To help you, the series distills the best of scholarly insights into the straightforward language and devotional emphasis of a daily Bible guide. Explanations of background material, and discussions of the original Greek and Hebrew, will always aim to be brief.

• If you have never really studied the Bible before, the series offers a serious yet accessible way in.

• If you help to lead a church study group, or are otherwise involved in regular preaching and teaching, you can find invaluable "snapshots" of a Bible passage through the DBC approach.

• If you are a church worker or minister, burned out on the Bible, this series could help you recover the wonder of scripture.

USING A DOUBLEDAY
BIBLE COMMENTARY

The series is designed for use alongside any version of the Bible. You may have your own favorite translation, but you might like to consider using a different one in order to gain fresh perspectives on familiar passages.

Many Bible translations come in a range of editions, including study and reference editions that have concordances, various special kinds of special indexes, maps, and marginal notes. These can all prove helpful in studying the relevant passage. The Notes section at the back of each DBC volume provides space for you to write personal reflections, points to follow up, questions, and comments.

Each Doubleday Bible Commentary can be used on a daily basis. Alternatively, it can be read straight through, or used as a resource book for insight into particular verses of the biblical book.

If you have enjoyed using this commentary and would like to progress further in Bible study, you will find details of other volumes in the series listed at the back.

While it is important to deepen understanding of a given passage, this series always aims to engage both heart and mind in the study of the Bible. The scriptures point to our Lord himself and our task is to use them to build our relationship with him. When we read, let us do so prayerfully, slowly, reverently, expecting him to speak to our hearts.

CONTENTS

INTRODUCTION

"I can't wait to read the end of the book"—how often have you said that? Sometimes we are tempted to take a quick look at the end when we are only halfway through! It goes without saying that the end of a book is important, often gripping, fascinating. For a novel, it's the climax of the story. If we look at it too soon, we lose the excitement and suspense. And if it is a detailed discussion on a technical matter, the end is often the place where the threads are drawn together and the results are set out clearly.

The Old Testament is a different matter—not so much a book, more a library, it is often said. And sadly, these last six short books, Nahum to Malachi, are often the volumes that are left to gather dust on the bookshelves. It seems to have been Augustine, back in the fourth century, who first described them as "minor prophets." He was not disparaging their importance, merely referring to their brevity compared with the major prophets, Isaiah, Jeremiah, and Ezekiel. For, with the exception of Zechariah, which has fourteen chapters, they are very short books indeed, ranging from Haggai with only two chapters to Malachi with four, and in the Hebrew Bible even Malachi has only three chapters. By the third century B.C. these six books formed a single scroll together with the six prophets from Hosea to Micah, and were known as the Book of the Twelve Prophets.

Our six prophets fall into two groups. Nahum, Habakkuk, and Zephaniah were active toward the end of the seventh century B.C., when the Assyrian Empire was in decline. It finally fell before the advance of the Babylonians in 612 B.C. In 587, Jerusalem itself was conquered by the Babylonians and the period known as the Exile began. By the time of Haggai, Zechariah, and Malachi, the Babylonian Empire, too, had fallen, defeated by the Persians. In 538, Cyrus, the Persian ruler, issued an edict allowing the Jews (and other nations) to return to their own lands. But the glorious, joyful hopes expressed in Isaiah 40–55 failed to materialize.

Apathy set in; there were tensions within society; the Jerusalem temple remained in ruins. Into this situation came two prophets, Haggai and Zechariah, both concerned with the rebuilding of the temple. The Bible neatly summarizes the results of their ministry: "The elders of the Jews built and prospered, through the prophesying of Haggai the prophet and Zechariah the son of Iddo" (Ezra 6:14). Between 520 and 515, the temple in Jerusalem was rebuilt. The date of Malachi is uncertain but is probably around 450 B.C.

The situation as far as the books are concerned, in contrast to the prophets themselves, is more complex. Even at a cursory reading it is clear that chapters 9–14 of Zechariah differ significantly from chapters 1–8 both in style and in content, and come from a much later period, probably the late fourth or early third century B.C. There are too few indicators within the text to enable us to pinpoint their date with any greater certainty. The early chapters of Zechariah, with their strange, even bizarre, visions, have some of the characteristics of what has come to be known as apocalyptic literature. In chapters 9–14 these characteristics are more fully developed.

Apocalyptic Literature

THE IMPORTANCE OF prophets gradually waned. Before the Exile, Isaiah and Jeremiah had been involved with kings and affairs of state. Even after the Exile, when the country was no longer an independent nation, Haggai and Zechariah had considerable influence in motivating the community to put worship at its heart. But gradually prophetic ministry declined, partly due to the fact that many prophecies remained unfulfilled. As we shall see in our study of Zechariah, the role of prophet fell into disrepute. Then came the rise of apocalyptic literature, which takes its name from a Greek word *(apokalyptein)* meaning "to reveal." The main examples in the Bible are Daniel in the Old Testament and Revelation in the New Testament, but there are other examples, among them Zechariah 9–14. Whereas the prophets expected God to intervene within history to right wrongs and bring justice, the apocalyptic writers thought in terms of a new age to come when God would establish his kingdom and, by direct intervention, would bring salvation. This type of literature flourished particularly in the period between the Old and New Testaments, from the second century B.C. to the first century A.D.

One Bible, Two Testaments

THE ORDER OF the books in the Christian Bible binds the Old and New Testaments into a single whole. Whereas the Hebrew Bible (the *Tanach*, to give it its Jewish name) ends with Chronicles and includes the prophets in the middle section, the Old Testament (as Christians call it) ends with Malachi, with a prophecy that looks forward to the future, pointing us to God's coming in Jesus and to his messenger, John the Baptist, a second Elijah (Matthew 11:13–14).

The Old Testament is not easy to read. Written in an ancient language, it comes from a society very different from ours. Yet we must avoid the temptation to read it only as if it were ancient history or ancient literature, fascinating but not relevant to our modern world. As holy scripture, it is God's word to us and we must allow it to speak with its own voice, often an uncomfortable and challenging voice despite all the centuries that have passed. For the Christian it is, of course, incomplete, awaiting its fulfillment in the coming of Jesus, the Messiah. In our study we shall look at the continuity of both the Old and New Testaments, showing that they are indeed one Bible, but we shall see also the contrasts between them that make the New Testament radically new.

Bible Versions

THE TRANSLATION ON which these studies are based is the New Revised Standard Version (NRSV), from which quotations are taken unless otherwise indicated. One sign of the vitality and relevance of the Bible today is the number of modern English translations produced in recent years. This is enriching but it also raises problems for the writing of notes and commentaries! The Good News Bible is especially helpful to readers unfamiliar with the Bible. Some versions, particularly the NRSV, its earlier form the Revised Standard (RSV), and the New International (NIV), follow the structure of the Hebrew and Greek closely, giving as far as is possible in translation the "feel" of the original. The New English Bible (NEB) and the Revised English Bible (REB) aim for more idiomatic English.

SUGGESTIONS FOR FURTHER READING

COMMENTARIES

Baldwin, J. *Haggai, Zechariah, Malachi*, Tyndale Old Testament Commentary, IVP, 1972.

Mason, R. *The Books of Haggai, Zechariah and Malachi*, Cambridge Bible Commentary, Cambridge, England, 1977.

Smith, R. L. *Micah–Malachi*, Word Biblical Commentary, Word, Waco, Texas, 1984.

Watts, J.D.W. *The Books of Joel, Obadiah, Jonah, Nahum, Habakkuk and Zephaniah*, Cambridge Bible Commentary, Cambridge, England, 1975.

OLD TESTAMENT GUIDES

Brief introductory volumes published by Sheffield Academic Press, Sheffield, England:

Coggins, R. J. *Haggai, Zechariah, Malachi*, 1987.

Mason, R. *Micah, Nahum, Obadiah*, 1991.

Mason, R. *Zephaniah, Habakkuk, Joel*, 1994.

FOR MORE ADVANCED STUDY

House, P. R. *Zephaniah: A Prophetic Drama*, Bible and Literature Series 16, Almond Press, Sheffield, England, 1989.

MINOR PROPHETS II

Nahum, Habakkuk, Zephaniah, Haggai, Zechariah, Malachi

JUDGMENT AND MERCY

THE BEGINNING OF Nahum is hardly an attractive invitation to read further. What kind of book is this to be found in the Bible? It seems to confirm the view that the God of the Old Testament is a God of vengeance, far removed from the loving Father whom we know from the New Testament. That, of course, is far too simplistic a contrast and untrue to both Old and New Testaments. Ironically, Nahum's name means "comfort," and we soon discover that his ominous words of judgment are shot through continually with glorious hope. To read the book as if its sole theme were bloodthirsty revenge is a gross distortion of the prophet's message and enables us to sidestep the continuing challenge of these ancient words. In fact, Nahum's purpose can be described as bringing comfort to Judah, a small country oppressed by the powerful nation of Assyria, whose capital city was Nineveh. The word "jealous," when used of God, signifies not a petty emotion but the closeness of his relationship to his people and the vulnerability of his love.

Nahum Among the Prophets

IT IS IMPORTANT when reading Nahum to remember that this little "book" does not stand alone but is part of the Book of the Twelve Prophets, which begins with Hosea and ends with Malachi. They are often referred to as the "minor prophets," that is, the shorter prophets in comparison with the long books of Isaiah, Jeremiah, and Ezekiel. In the Book of the Twelve, judgment and mercy are counterbalanced; there is judgment for all, including Israel, and mercy for all, including Nineveh.

The Historical Setting

ASSYRIA WAS ONE of the great international powers of the eighth and seventh centuries B.C. It was the Assyrians who overthrew the northern kingdom, Israel, in 722 B.C. and overran its territory. Judah, too, suffered the brutality of Assyria's military might. By Nahum's time, however, Assyria itself was threatened by other rising powers, and in 612 B.C. Nineveh was captured by the Medes. Nahum's words are probably to be dated shortly before that time. Rather than gloating over a conquered enemy, they are a cry for help by people still desperate for relief from tyrannical oppression and from savage acts of war against the helpless. It isn't necessary to read back into history to get the feel of this. Our newspapers and TV screens confront us daily with similar atrocities. Viewed in this light, Nahum can be understood rather than condemned. His words are an affirmation of faith in God's sovereignty and his power to save, in the face of human brutality.

The Message

HUMAN SUFFERING MATTERS to God. Those who destroy lives and shatter happiness are in the end accountable to him. Deliverance for the oppressed means judgment on the oppressor. But Nahum knows that this is not the whole story. In spite of rampant evil, God is patient—"slow to anger," says Nahum.

God is not an unjust judge. The guilty will not go unpunished, their crimes disregarded. And isn't justice precisely what we long for in our unjust world? This is what the book of Nahum is about.

A Thought for Today

"THE LORD WILL by no means clear the guilty." Did Paul perhaps have these words of Nahum's in mind when he wrestled with the problem of how God, just and holy as he is, can forgive us who have sinned? When he wrote to the Christians in Rome he had the answer: "By the free gift of God's grace all are put right with him through Christ Jesus, who sets them free" (Romans 3:24, GNB).

PRAYER

Thanks be to you, my Lord Jesus Christ, for all the pains and insults you have borne for me.

GOD OF DARKNESS AND STORM

NAHUM IS A book of powerful poetry, of "vision" as the title informs us, a kaleidoscope of rapidly changing pictures, not a literal account of events. The first verses are known as an acrostic, in which each line begins with a consecutive letter of the alphabet, in this case only half the alphabet.

Nahum's God is a majestic God, wholly other than humankind:

> *His way is in whirlwind and storm,*
> *and the clouds are the dust of his feet.*

Here is both the mystery and the power of God, the Almighty. Yet God is not thereby remote from us, for these are words to bring comfort in times of overwhelming, inexplicable sorrow, when all is darkness and even God seems to be hidden. But be assured, he is with us in the storm, he has not left us alone. Nahum's faith can be our faith too, and for us those "feet" are the feet of the crucified one. It was from out of a whirlwind that God spoke to Job in the midst of his suffering and anguished questioning, and Job was able to say, "I had heard of you by the hearing of the ear, but now my eye sees you" (Job 42:5). From secondhand report to firsthand encounter with the living God!

If verse 4 seems destructive, it also reminds us of God's great saving action when he rescued the Israelites from slavery in Egypt, drying up the sea so that they could cross on dry land. This story is to be found in Exodus 14:21–22.

Rejoice, the Lord Is King

NAHUM'S POETRY IS reminiscent of some of the psalms, and if we set it alongside Psalm 97, we shall see that "cloud and darkness" spell not gloom but mystery. Psalm 97 is, after all, a resounding celebration of God as king, a psalm overflowing with joy for all to share: "Let the earth rejoice" (v. 1). But true worship requires also an element of mystery:

Clouds and thick darkness are all around him;
righteousness and justice are the foundation of his throne.

PSALM 97:2

Like Nahum, the psalmist, too, attributes the great cataclysms of nature to God's awesome power: The earth trembles, mountains melt like wax before his presence. Here is a reminder for us that the God who is so close as to be called "our Father," whose love provided the Savior, is not to be treated lightly, as if he were a god made in human image: He is king, Lord of all, an awesome presence. Making himself vulnerable in Christ on the cross, he is not encompassed by the limits of our world. On both counts, his love and his majesty, he is a God worthy of all worship.

PRAYER

Lord, when we cannot feel your presence, grant us the faith to believe that you are ever beside us and that your purpose is always grounded in your love. Lift up our hearts in the midst of the whirlwinds and storms of our lives and lead us into worship and praise.

THE LORD IS GOOD

NAHUM SHOWS US the two "faces" of God—his anger against sin and his care for the troubled. Notice, it is not his care for the *good*, as though humans needed to strive hard after virtue in order to secure God's favor. True, there is no easy offer of comfort for those who deliberately turn from what is good, but the sole qualification for God's protection in time of trouble is that trusting attitude that "takes refuge in him" (v. 7). Here is a great word of hope, a promise from God himself. He is good, and that sums up all that follows—a stronghold, a protection, a refuge in any and every time of distress. And all we need to do is to trust, to take refuge in him.

Plotting Against the Lord

ALTHOUGH THE HEADING of the book (v. 1) focuses on Nineveh, Nahum's thoughts range more widely. He is concerned with evil on a massive scale, not simply with Nineveh's brutality, notorious though that was even in the ancient world. For Nahum, the visionary, Nineveh is symbolic of cosmic evil, against which the Lord pits his might to avenge the wretched victims of inhuman oppression. When we pray, "Thy will be done on earth as in heaven," we are praying for the overthrow of evil in the world, for the defeat of all that defies God and tramples on his love. Our words are poles apart from Nahum's, but our longing is the same. Nahum doesn't pull his punches: Evil, he says bluntly, is nothing other than plotting against the Lord. And isn't this a fair description of some of the rampant, hideous evil our TV screens confront us with? Nahum's images are vivid; one can almost hear the crackling flames as they lick around the dry straw. Nahum's words, though offensive, sharpen our sensitivities, blunted as they sometimes are by overexposure, at a safe and sanitized distance, to the ills that millions are suffering this very day.

God's Victory over "Belial"

THIS SECTION CONCLUDES in verse 11 with a very somber word. Again Nahum's words are nonspecific: No enemy is identified, although in some translations you will find the word "Nineveh" inserted. But Nahum has in mind not simply a historic enemy but evil personified. This is clearer in the original Hebrew than in some English translations. The Revised English Bible comes closest with its rendering "a wicked counselor," but the word for "wicked" is also a personal name in Hebrew and the phrase can equally well be translated "the counselor Belial"—a seductive and insidious being, inciting to evil. Nahum was aware that there is a demonic element in evil, not explicable in purely human terms. The Hebrew word "Belial" is retained in the King James Version, for example, in describing the inhuman depravity exemplified in the sordid story of Judges 19:22–25. In modern versions, Belial is translated in Judges 19:22 by expressions such as "depraved," "wicked," or "perverted." Paul, with his Hebrew background, uses the same word when he illustrates the utter incompatibility of good and evil: "What fellowship has light with darkness? What accord has Christ with Belial?" (2 Corinthians 6:15) Here some modern versions, too, retain the Hebrew word, whereas the Good News Bible interprets it as "the Devil." But Nahum knows that no evil, however barbarous, is too powerful for the Lord.

A HYMN OF GOD'S TRIUMPH
Death's mightiest powers have done their worst,
And Jesus hath his foes dispersed,
Let shouts of praise and joy outburst.
Alleluia!

From the hymn "The Strife Is O'er," translated from the seventeenth-century Latin by the Reverend F. Potts, 1859.

7

VICTORY BELONGS TO THE LORD!

HERE FOR THE first time Nahum declares the authority behind his words: "Thus says the Lord." The one whose word Nahum speaks is the Lord who takes action on behalf of those who suffer. Here, too, threats of judgment against the tyrant are interspersed with promises of deliverance for the helpless. For more than a hundred years Judah had been subjugated by Assyria, burdened with heavy tribute, invaded and looted by Assyrian troops. The situation is not difficult for us to imagine, nor is the anguished cry for deliverance. There is, says the prophet, no future for oppressive power such as Nineveh symbolized; nor for worship of such as Ishtar, goddess of violence and war; nor for anything that would bring chaos and darkness back into the world where God has created order and light.

It was customary in the ancient world for the wealthy and for leaders to prepare their own impressive graves as a memorial for the future. But the evil enemy is depicted here in verse 14 as too weak and of too "little account" (REB—the Hebrew word means "trivial, lightweight") to build his own grave. This is Nahum's way of speaking of the ultimate humiliation of those who arrogantly plot against the living God.

Come, Let Us Celebrate

IMMEDIATELY AFTER THE darkness comes the bright hope that is God's purpose for us all. Look up, Nahum says, to the path over the mountains and watch the messenger running with good news—the battle is over, peace is won. The scene was familiar to Nahum's audience. It was just such a messenger, running with tragic news, that caused the death of the old priest Eli when he fell backward from the bench he was sitting on and broke his neck. The scene is lost to us in the immediacy of the telephone, fax, and e-mail, but the joyful relief when the waiting is over and good news has come is still the same. "Celebrate," says the prophet, and real celebration involves giving thanks to the Lord. Don't forget to worship, and don't forget to keep the promises you made to God when you pleaded for his help. Here is a reminder for us. We pray in trouble; do we sometimes forget to give thanks when all is well?

As we read Nahum in the light of the gospel and the tragedies of our world, we shall understand his confrontation with evil and his affirmation of God's sovereignty. For us this has a sharper focus; we have the cross of Jesus and his resurrection as clear signs of God's undefeated love. And so with confidence we pray, as Jesus taught us:

Deliver us from evil,
For thine is the kingdom,
the power, and the glory,
forever and ever.

MEDITATION

Read and rejoice in Psalm 91 and let it lead you to humble trust and worship. Notice particularly how it ends, not with a description of God's love, but with his direct promise:

Those who love me, I will deliver;
I will protect those who know my name.
When they call to me, I will answer them;
I will be with them in trouble,
I will rescue them and honor them.
With long life I will satisfy them,
and show them my salvation.

THE DESTROYER DESTROYED

NAHUM SPEAKS OF what he knows: his language is militaristic; he tells of war, violence, and pillage. But his thought is not limited to the literal and the historical. He sees beyond the fate threatening Nineveh to the God whose ultimate triumph overthrows all that is evil and that wars against the good. His words are to be understood in perspective as with sensitivity we enter into their meaning.

> *Let God rise up, let his enemies be scattered;*
> *let those who hate him flee before him . . .*
> *But let the righteous be joyful;*
> *let them exult before God.*

These words from Psalm 68:1 and 3 help us to put Nahum 2 into perspective.

Vision and Reality

THE CHAPTER BEGINS with a vivid battle scene, a siege with battering ram and troops mustering outside a city. The historical is interwoven with the visionary. Nahum is speaking of the fate soon to befall Israel's ruthless enemy, Nineveh, but he thinks, too, on a grander scale, in symbolic terms, of God's victory over all that is evil, as the psalm quoted above indicates. The literal and the symbolic are woven together. It is significant that Nineveh's name rarely appears; after the title it is not mentioned until 2:8 (despite its introduction earlier in some translations, making specific what Nahum himself leaves unspecified).

In your imagination, picture the scene. Far removed though it is from modern warfare, the violence, the fear, the despair, and the triumph of the victors are repeated around the world today. Circumstances change but human emotions are universal. Nahum's world has many points of contact with ours—too many. Today's marvelous achievements have not lessened the fear of war.

Behind the Battle, the Lord

THE SIEGE IS in progress. Some of the details are true to history—leather shields reddened with a substance known as reddle (red ochre) used for preservation and added strength, scarlet-clad warriors, chariots glittering in the sunlight, cavalry charging through the outskirts of the city, and shelters set up to protect the attacking forces from missiles thrown from the walls. But even while he speaks in literal terms of ancient warfare, of the Medes and Babylonians soon to overthrow Nineveh, Nahum, the visionary, sees beyond the immediate to a greater reality. The flashing chariots call to his mind the flash of forked lightning, a traditional image for the display of God's power in the forces of nature. But even in the midst of this battle scene we are reminded that God's judgment is always the prelude to salvation, that defeat of the destroyer is the necessary concomitant of help for the helpless.

God as a warrior is depicted elsewhere in the Old Testament, not because God himself is thought of as violent or as the instigator of war, but because in a world of violence and bloodshed, of power defined in military terms, God's supreme power is an article of faith.

AN AFFIRMATION OF FAITH
So be it, Lord; thy throne shall never,
Like earth's proud empires, pass away;
Thy kingdom stands and grows forever,
Till all thy creatures own thy sway.

From the hymn "The Day Thou Gavest, Lord, Is Ended" by John Ellerton (1826–93)

Chaos Controlled

At last, in verse 8, the name of the city is mentioned, the first time since the title. The battle scene continues; after the clash of arms comes the despair of the captives, the devastation of the city, and the plunder of its wealth, the tragic fate of many a city both ancient and modern. The sluice gates are opened, floods of water undermine the foundations, and buildings collapse. But the language has profound overtones reaching far beyond the literal. Once again the prophet speaks in both literal and symbolic terms. The enemy on the historical plane is Nineveh. On the visionary level it is Ishtar, the Assyrian goddess of immorality and violence, and behind Ishtar is the watery Chaos ("the deep" of Genesis 1:2), represented in ancient Israelite tradition as a monster (sometimes called Rahab) that was conquered by God at creation, its devastating floods continually restrained by his mighty hand. The language has profound overtones of God the creator and God the destroyer. The mighty cosmic ocean was restrained by God at creation so that dry land might appear; the same waters were unleashed by him at the flood in the time of Noah to do their work of destruction. A glimpse of this symbolic language can be seen in Psalm 89:8–10:

> *O Lord God of hosts,*
> *who is as mighty as you, O Lord?*
> *Your faithfulness surrounds you.*
> *You rule the raging of the sea;*
> *when its waves rise, you still them.*
> *You crushed Rahab (the Chaos monster) like a carcass;*
> *you scattered your enemies with your mighty arm.*

Light in a Dark World

The picture of the devastating floods sweeping the city suggests to the prophet the imagery that follows. The stream of captives is like a river flowing out of the city. Taken as slaves, they moan in despair, and mingling with these sorrowful sounds one hears the jubilation of the victors as they plunder the city's vast treasuries. But Nahum's thought is not solely of historical conquest, urgent though that is for Judah's relief from Assyrian oppression. He rejoices in the confidence of God's ultimate triumph over all that destroys life and human happiness.

Assyrian power had long since gone when Jesus was born. It was the Roman Empire that then held sway. But it was still a world of strife and oppression, of occupying armies, when Jesus came as a light into the world. Light is more powerful than darkness; "the light shines in the darkness," says John's Gospel, "and the darkness did not overcome it" (John 1:5).

Evil must be taken seriously, but so must the cross, where God turned tragedy into triumph. And in Jesus' words, "Father, forgive," the light still shines, illuminating the darkness and pointing the only way to future hope.

FOR MEDITATION

Read Psalm 93. Join the psalmist in celebrating God as king, and rejoice in his ultimate control of the forces of chaos, whatever they may be, which still threaten to consume our world. And let us take to heart the challenge of verse 5:

Your decrees are very sure;
holiness befits your house,
O Lord, forevermore.

DEVASTATION AFTER CONQUEST

"DEVASTATION, DESOLATION, AND destruction"—the repetition of these similar-sounding words is an attempt to reproduce the carefully structured Hebrew with its doom-laden sounds ascending to an ominous climax *(buqah umebuqah umebulaqah)*. The description of sheer terror and agitation is a literal portrayal of the shock and terror of defeat. The language used is powerful: "Knees tremble, all loins quake, all faces grow pale." All Nineveh's strength has gone. If this kindles our own concern and sympathy, how much more does it call forth God's compassion?

With powerful imagery the prophet poignantly highlights the contrast between former greatness and imminent disaster. The lion symbolizes not only Nineveh's strength but its apparently unassailable security—the lion's cubs are hidden in its lair with none to frighten or disturb them. And with an abundance of prey for food, their future looks secure. But the image of the lion has other overtones particularly appropriate to this chapter. For Nahum is concerned not merely with human enemies and human brutality. As a prophet, bringing God's word to bear on the situation, he sees on a deeper level the demonic evil that incites humans to betray their humanity, and by their foul deeds to deny that they were created in God's image. For Nahum, in his particular generation, this evil was embodied in Ishtar, goddess of violence and immorality, and in the Chaos monster, God's adversary in creation. And in ancient Near Eastern art Ishtar is represented sometimes mounted on a lion or as herself a lioness, and the Chaos monster, too, is depicted as a lion.

The last words of the chapter are somber: "I am against you, says the Lord of hosts." No amount of chariotry and military might can withstand the Lord. Yet Israel, too, had to learn the lesson of where true power lies. Tempted to rely for help on the tangible and visible, and not on the unseen yet ever-present Lord, they were warned by another prophet, a century before Nahum:

Alas for those who go down to Egypt for help
and who rely on horses,
who trust in chariots because they are many
and in horsemen because they are very strong,
but do not look to the Holy One of Israel
or consult the Lord!
. . . The Egyptians are human, and not God;
their horses are flesh, and not spirit.

ISAIAH 31:1, 3

FOR MEDITATION

Nahum's words are an affirmation of faith, faith in God's power
to subdue evil and deliver the helpless. But for faith there is always a
tension between the "now" and the "not yet." The Lord is king,
yet still we pray:

Thy kingdom come, O God,
Thy rule, O Christ, begin,
Break with thine iron rod
The tyrannies of sin.

From the hymn "Thy Kingdom Come" by Canon Lewis Hensley, 1867

REAPING DUE REWARD

HERE IS A horrific picture of battle and its aftermath. The chapter does not make pleasant reading. But we must be careful not to misread. The scene of devastation, the noise of battle, whips cracking, chariot wheels rumbling, swords flashing, and finally the silence of death, "heaps of corpses, dead bodies without end," are not God's doing. They are descriptive of Nineveh's acts of violence, "city of bloodshed, full of booty." And behind all this, inciting to evil, is the worship of Ishtar, goddess of immoral sex and violence. Although the goddess is not mentioned by name, the strongly sexual terms the prophet uses to depict Nineveh's debauchery (vv. 4–5) make the allusion to Ishtar unmistakable. We become like that which we worship, and this was true of Nineveh in its worship of such a violent goddess. But how true is it of us who worship the God of compassion and love?

The prophet's thought extends beyond the wrong done to his own people to include a concern for other nations that Nineveh has enslaved. This is evil on a massive scale. Yet there is one with whom Nineveh has not reckoned—the Lord of hosts, Lord of all the earth.

The Destroyer Destroyed

THE DESCRIPTION OF Nineveh's humiliation is offensive. The language of exposure, reflecting possibly a practice of the time, is not uncommon in the prophets Hosea, Jeremiah, and Ezekiel. The city that enslaved and degraded "nations through her debaucheries, and peoples through her sorcery" will itself suffer shame and humiliation. But there is no one to lament its fate, so hated and feared has it become. In the broad sweep of history, evil does not go unpunished, affirms the prophet. Nineveh, city of bloodshed, has been guilty of many innocent deaths; it has been enriched through the plundering of others, its territories increased at the cost of many deaths. The prophet piles accusation upon accusation: Nineveh is deceitful, seductive, enslaving. Yet the victims of this brutal oppression are to be avenged and judgment meted out to the oppressor.

God's Final Reckoning

NAHUM'S LAST CHAPTER is darkness with no gleam of light. It is more somber than the previous chapters, horrific though they were. It speaks only of doom and death, moving at times from the literal realities of ancient warfare to figurative portrayals of helpless disaster. But his intention is not to revel in images of brutality and ruthless hostility. He is speaking of the seriousness of trifling with God. Nineveh's name has appeared only rarely throughout the book, and when it does it is a symbol of far greater evil, that cosmic evil that Nahum, drawing on the ancient mythology we have met already in Psalm 89, visualizes as the Chaos monster, the Creator's primeval foe. Give it what name we will, it is as evident in our world as it was in Nahum's. It is a greater, more powerful evil than the sum of human sin. God's judgment falls on those who flout his will for justice, peace, and love, of whatever race they may be. Israel, too, was reminded time and time again by the prophets that none is exempt from accountability to God.

PRAYER

Lord, grant that amid the rampant evil of the world we may never lose heart, but draw our strength from you, our Rock and our Redeemer.

A Lesson from History

NAHUM ILLUSTRATES THE transience of all human power by a lesson drawn from Assyria's own annals. Thebes (called by its Hebrew name No-Amon), a great Egyptian city situated on the Nile, fell to the Assyrians in 663 B.C. despite all its wealth and security, and its notable allies among the strong nations adjacent to it (Put is probably Somalia). The description of Thebes "with water around her, her rampart a sea, water her wall," is poetic exaggeration rather than factual description, mythology rather than geography. In Egyptian eyes Thebes was a sacred city, reputed to have been founded on the dry land that was the first to emerge from the primeval waters at creation.

In the same way shall powerful Nineveh fall. But Nahum's perspective is different from that of the Assyrians recorded in their annals. For the prophet, the downfall of Thebes signals not the achievements of Assyria's military forces but the fragility of earthly powers. Nahum's thought moves from the dread realities of defeat and the horrific picture he paints of the sack of Thebes to figurative language describing Assyria's threatened fate. His imagery is vivid:

> *All your fortresses are like fig trees*
> *with first ripe figs—*
> *if shaken they fall*
> *into the mouth of the eater (v. 12).*

Nineveh's defeated troops are disparaged in what to us are offensive terms: "They are women in your midst," says the prophet (v. 13). This demeaning reference to women reflects the patriarchal society that ancient Israel was, and sadly this strand is found in various ways in several other prophets. The Old Testament as a whole, it must be said, gives women an honorable place, not least in its affirmation that both man and woman are made in the image of God and both alike are set as the guardians of the created world.

No Place to Hide

ASSYRIA WILL BE open and unprotected against the enemy just as surely as a city whose gates have been burned down. Fortresses, troops, gates, all such material sources of security, are in the end a sham. Ironically the prophet echoes the desperate instructions of those who try in vain to ward off the attackers in the last desperate preparations to withstand the siege. Water is drawn and stored for future need, clay is trampled, mud bricks are shaped in the mold, but all is a futile defense against the enemy that will consume them as thoroughly as locusts destroy crops. Nahum's thought lingers on that word "locust." The enemy will consume them like locusts, even if their troops should multiply at the speed of locusts. What could be a more telling image of devastation than this for those who knew from their own experience the silent, swift descent of a swarm of locusts!

The prophet speaks of unrelieved doom, of brutal acts perpetrated against the helpless rebounding upon the perpetrator. But implicit in his words is the eternal hope that "victory belongs to the Lord."

FOR MEDITATION

Let this be recorded for a generation to come,
so that a people yet unborn may praise the Lord:
that he looked down from his holy height,
from heaven the Lord looked at the earth,
to hear the groans of the prisoners,
to set free those who were doomed to die.

PSALM 102:18–20

THE SLEEP OF DEATH

NAHUM'S WORDS OF doom continue. Yes, you did multiply, says the prophet, your merchants became more numerous than the stars of heaven. But his thought still lingers around that powerful, destructive image of the locusts and grasshoppers. His words are double-edged. Innumerable these insects may be, but they swarm, here one moment, gone the next, dependent on the vagaries of the weather. The image of locusts sitting on a fence in the cold, suddenly warmed by the sun into activity, and gone no one knows where, could be a picturesque image if it did not convey so doom-laden a message. The prophet drives home his words with image piled on image: shepherds, that is nobles, asleep, oblivious alike to their responsibilities and to the threatening danger. The people are like sheep scattered over the hillsides with no one to control and tend them, leaderless and at the mercy of marauders. And still there is more. The doom is complete, the wound beyond healing. The sleep is the sleep of death. And last of all comes the reason for this terrible portrayal of inescapable judgment, the reason why God is depicted as the avenger in the opening verses of the book. No tears will be shed over Nineveh's demise; her cruelty to conquered foes was total and unremitting. It was, says the Hebrew literally, "evil without end." With these words the book of Nahum ends.

The descriptive poetry is magnificent and its challenge is inescapable. Evil brings its own reward. Oppression works isolation for the oppressor; the din of violence issues in the silence of death. The one who remains amid the wreckage of history is the Lord, whose will is justice for the oppressed.

A Book Within a Book

NAHUM IS NOT to be read in isolation as if God's final word was ever one of defeat. It is part of the Book of the Twelve, and is followed immediately by Habakkuk, whose words end on an up beat—"I will rejoice in the Lord;

I will exult in the God of my salvation"—and by Zephaniah, who pictures God rejoicing over his people "with loud singing as on a day of festival."

Evil does not triumph. God is not defeated, as the cross and resurrection of Jesus remind us. The apostle Paul, many centuries after Nahum, recognized the same cosmic evil, greater than the sum of human sin, "the spiritual forces of evil" against which he and his fellow Christians had to contend. But he had a remedy, and so do we:

Finally, be strong in the Lord and in the strength of his power. Put on the whole armor of God, so that you may be able to stand against the wiles of the devil.

EPHESIANS 6:10–11

AN OLD TESTAMENT PROMISE.
MAY IT BRIGHTEN TODAY FOR US!
The Lord loves those who hate evil;
he guards the lives of his faithful;
he rescues them from the hand of the wicked.
Light dawns for the righteous,
and joy for the upright in heart.
Rejoice in the Lord, O you righteous,
and give thanks to his holy name!

PSALM 97:10–12

A DIALOGUE WITH GOD

WHAT A CONTRAST the beginning of Habakkuk is to Nahum! There we needed imaginative sensitivity to enter into Nahum's situation in order to understand his violent outburst. Here in Habakkuk we sense that we have found a kindred spirit to ourselves, a prophet who has felt like we do, who has known the heartache and bewilderment of life, who has kept on praying even though God didn't seem to answer. And isn't it so with us? Life is bewildering in its tragedies and disappointments, and we cry out for an explanation, something to make sense of disaster and of God's apparent silence.

The prophet with the strange-sounding name (it is unusual, too, in Hebrew) lived probably toward the end of the seventh century B.C. and was more or less contemporary with Nahum, perhaps a little younger. In Habakkuk's time the Assyrian Empire was already crumbling and a new power, Babylon (modern Iraq), was in the ascendant.

Habakkuk serves as a counterbalance to Nahum, a reminder that the God of justice has no favorites. He calls to account not only foreign nations but his own people, Judah. Nahum may have seemed to us rather nationalistic. Habakkuk reminds us that God's people, too, are responsible for their actions. The righteous God will not tolerate evil among his people. Both prophets alike affirm God's sovereignty in history, though Nahum is concerned with the overthrow of a foreign aggressor and Habakkuk with the problems of Judah's own society, where the powerful were oppressing the weak.

A Puzzled Prophet

THIS IS A very personal book. It shows the prophet in his intimate dealings with God. But as a prophet, Habakkuk was also voicing the distress and bewilderment of the people. Here is a prophet who believes that God is powerful to right the wrongs suffered by the weak and oppressed, if only he will take action. But there lies the problem: God seems silent and inactive. And so the book starts with an outspoken complaint by the prophet. There is no hesitancy, no beating about the bush. The prophet is blunt. He has been praying, calling on God, but so far no answer has come. All around are violence and strife; society is convulsed; the law is ineffective and the law courts perverted. The identities of the wicked and the righteous are uncertain. Probably Habakkuk has in mind the Assyrian rulers and their Judean collaborators who oppress the faithful among God's people. There is no justice to avenge the suffering. Who can help but God—and he is doing nothing.

Yet the prophet still believes. His faith is troubled, but it holds fast, and in his bewilderment he brings his complaint to this same silent, seemingly inactive God. For Israel's God is his only hope—of this, Habakkuk is sure.

MEDITATION
Read and rejoice in Psalm 62:6–7, 11–12:

He alone is my rock and my salvation,
my fortress; I shall not be shaken.
On God rests my deliverance and my honor;
my mighty rock, my refuge is in God . . .
Once God has spoken;
twice have I heard this:
that power belongs to God,
and steadfast love belongs to you, O Lord.

God's Strange Answer

THE PROPHET HAS prayed in the name of the people and on their behalf. Now he speaks in God's name, for the prophets had a dual role as God's messengers, to bring his word to his people, and as intercessors, to bring the people's needs before God. God's answer to Habakkuk's complaint is indirect, if indeed it is intended to be an answer at all. In fact it becomes just another source of bewilderment to the prophet.

The Lord of History

THE MESSAGE COMES to Habakkuk that God is in control, but what does he mean by "rousing the Chaldeans (the Babylonians), that fierce and impetuous nation," and what is his aim? Elsewhere in the Old Testament, when God uses a foreign nation to fulfill his purposes, the reason is explained. The Assyrians in Isaiah's time became the agents of judgment on God's people, Israel. During the Exile in Babylon, Cyrus, the Persian ruler, was instrumental in restoring the exiled Israelites to their homeland. God works in history both in judgment and in salvation. But Habakkuk is bewildered. It was injustice at home that troubled him. Now, in response, he hears of frightening movements of troops abroad. "Where is God in all this?" he wonders, as so many people did during the Holocaust of the mid-twentieth century. But notice what God says: "Look . . . and see." Don't keep too narrow a focus. Faith needs wider vision, not concentration on our own immediate problems to the exclusion of all else. There is evidence of God at work in the world if only we look for it. And so he broadens the prophet's vision.

The rising power of the Babylonians on the international stage spelled the downfall of the mighty Assyrian Empire and its capital, Nineveh, with which Nahum had been concerned. Assyria was defeated finally in 609 B.C. and the Babylonian Empire held sway. Their powerful and brutal forces are described here in striking imagery, for Habakkuk is both a visionary and a poet. Yet, mighty as are the Babylonian armies and terrifying in the swiftness of their conquests, they are under God's control: "*I am rousing* . . ." says the Lord to his prophet. The initiative is his alone. But the Babylonians offer their worship and devotion to another: "their own might is their god!"

Of His Kingdom There Shall Be No End

GOD'S ANSWER TO Habakkuk's prayer seems a strange kind of encouragement to the fragmented, unstable society on whose behalf the prophet has been pleading. Yet it is an affirmation of the truth we do well to remember, that God is sovereign and human minds cannot fathom the mystery of his ways. On the world scene, nation destroys nation, empires rise and fall. Amid the wreckage of time God's kingdom alone remains, a kingdom founded not on military might but on vulnerable love.

The apostle Paul had read this chapter and, when he was preaching in the synagogue at Antioch in Pisidia at sabbath worship, he quoted some of Habakkuk's words as they appear in the early Greek translation (the Septuagint). Paul's subject was this: "By this Jesus everyone who believes is set free from all those sins from which you could not be freed by the law of Moses" (Acts 13:39). Beware, says Paul, don't scoff . . . "for in your days I am doing a work, a work that you will never believe, even if someone tells you" (Acts 13:41).

A THOUGHT

God's work for us through Christ is amazing; indeed it is beyond belief—
unless he opens our eyes and gives us the insight of faith.

13 HABAKKUK 1:12–17

THE PROPHET CHALLENGES GOD

HABAKKUK STILL HASN'T received an answer to his questions. Indeed, the situation seems to have grown worse for, as time has passed, the brutality of the Babylonians has become even more notorious. And so he challenges God again with question after question. He starts with the traditional expressions of worship. God is eternal, holy, and immortal; he is a "Rock," a familiar expression in the psalms for protection and stability. But how do these affirmations of faith fit with the reality he sees around him? How can the holy God use the wicked to fulfill his purposes? Is it not a denial of his very nature? Yet Habakkuk is a believer, though a troubled one, and his doubts are voiced to the one whom he can still address as "Lord my God." His is a personal relationship with the Holy One.

Habakkuk paints a vivid picture with his figurative language. In their ruthless pursuit of further conquests, the Babylonians are as indiscriminate as fishermen trawling for fish. They empty their net time after time, only to take yet more captives, people whose forced labor will bring wealth and renown to Babylon. And the instruments of war that make them rich have become their gods to whom they offer worship. In the face of their relentless approach, the people are as defenseless and as leaderless as the fish of the ocean. From God's perspective there may be a purpose in all this; from Habakkuk's point of view the advance of the Babylonians seems as random as trawling for fish. Before their advancing armies, not only Israel but other nations face destruction "without mercy."

The Freedom to Question

THE OLD TESTAMENT is never hesitant to question God. The psalmists are bold in their approach, and so is Job. Here is encouragement for us to be open with God about the things that trouble us, the awkward questions that test our faith. He is, after all, the one "to whom all hearts are open, all desires known, and from whom no secrets are hidden." When we agonize over the problem of how faith and reality can coexist in this troubled world, let us lay hold on God, mindful as Habakkuk was that, despite all the problems, he is still "my God," the one to whom I have committed myself. God does not confuse doubt with blasphemy. It was, after all, Job's anguished questions that received God's approval, not the superficial conventional piety of his "friends." And Jesus, too, in his direst moments questioned God: "My God, why hast thou forsaken me?" To close our eyes to problems, to make God and his ways fit into our preconceived ideas, is not faith but timid self-defense. It is, in short, self-deception.

And so Habakkuk's challenge to God ends with an unanswered question. How can he square what he sees in the world around with his belief in a God of justice? Habakkuk must wait in patience. His journey from fear to faith has only just begun.

PRAYER
Grant, Lord, that we may never look complacently at the world's suffering, but bring our perplexity and doubts to you who are, today and always, our God.

THE RIGHTEOUS LIVE BY THEIR FAITH

The Prophet's Task

THESE VERSES GIVE an insight into the demands of the prophet's role. It was not an easy task. He has challenged God for the second time with his complaint on the people's behalf. Now he must watch and wait patiently for the answer. In his own time God answers, but only then, as Jeremiah also discovered. The message was God's; it was not at the prophet's disposal—not an easy lesson for Jeremiah to learn when confronted by false prophets who challenged the validity of his message and the authenticity of his calling (Jeremiah 28:10). And not easy for Habakkuk either, with injustice rampant and danger threatening, to watch and wait patiently.

Prophets as Watchmen

A FAMILIAR DESCRIPTION of prophets in the Old Testament is "watchmen." The watchman on the city walls looked carefully and attentively for evidence of approaching danger or, in times of siege, for possible signs of help to come. God's watchman, the prophet, is alert for God's word, which must be brought to bear on the existing situation, whether it be a promise of salvation or a word of warning. In the book of Ezekiel (chapter 33) there is a solemn charge to the prophet-watchman. If he fulfills his task, despite the hostility of his hearers, he is guiltless of what may befall them. But if he fails to warn them, whether through cowardice or negligence, their blood will be upon him; he will bear the guilt. The task of a prophet was not for the apathetic or the squeamish. They were charged with the solemn responsibility to be the spokespeople of God.

The News Published

AT LAST HABAKKUK gets his answer. The wicked (probably the Babylonians are in mind but the word is relevant more widely to other situations) will get their just deserts. Though judgment may be delayed, it will surely come, in God's own time—God's answer. It is to be written plainly in large letters so that all can read it at a glance, even someone who is running by. It is still the practice today in China and some eastern countries for news to be displayed in public places for all to read. Or we might think of the billboards in our streets where headline news may be placarded.

Habakkuk's message from God is brief and clear: There is no future for the arrogant, but the righteous (that is, those who live according to God's righteousness) will live by their faithfulness. And faithfulness means continual commitment to God, the long-term, quiet perseverance on the basis of trust in God and his good purposes, a matter of faith, not sight. There is a tension between promise and fulfillment for Habakkuk and his contemporaries. And so it has been throughout the ages. We, too, need to hold on to the promises of God in patient waiting for his fulfillment. But patient waiting does not mean listless apathy or quiet indifference. It means active commitment to the kingdom.

Habakkuk's words express for Paul the heart of the gospel, that faith is the essential basis of our life with God, whether in time or in eternity. We are justified by faith in Christ, which doesn't start with *anything* we do, but must affect and change *everything* we do (Romans 3:21–24).

PRAYER
Lord, as we wait for the coming of your kingdom of peace and love, renew our energies and strengthen our wills to serve you faithfully in your church and in your world.

GREED AND AVARICE CONDEMNED

THE REMAINDER OF the chapter consists of a series of "woes," five in all, against those who, in their various ways, are responsible for the sorrows of others. "Woe to you . . ." (NIV) conveys the meaning more strongly than "alas . . ." It is not so much a lament over evil as a forthright announcement of God's commitment to overthrow injustice wherever it is found, for it is an infringement of his sovereign rule and an attack on the very foundation of his kingdom. God is, as Psalm 99 affirms, "Mighty King, lover of justice."

The "woes" are directed against different categories of wrongdoing: first, in verses 6–8, against the greedy in society who pile up wealth to which they are not entitled and heap up riches at the expense of others. This is in effect theft and robbery, and it involves violence and fraud.

Here is the same sympathy for the weak and powerless that motivated the prophet's complaints to God in chapter 1. But now he not only pleads for their relief but calls down judgment on the guilty, to the end that ruthlessness and greed may be obliterated from society. Some of the wealth has been amassed from goods taken in pledge, given as security for loans, and never returned to their rightful owners, in blatant defiance of Israelite law, which had strict regulations to protect the poor from exploitation. But the plunderer will himself be plundered, says the prophet, whether his wealth has been gained through the unjust structures of society or extorted on a grander scale in international affairs, as the end of this section suggests. Both individuals and nations alike are accountable to God, who is concerned with injustice wherever it is perpetrated. He has no favorites. Nor, as the Almighty, is he in thrall to any earthly power, however impressive.

But the prophet has still further accusations to bring against the avaricious. They are guilty not only of human bloodshed but of violence done to the earth itself in the plundering of its resources, an ecological issue dear to our hearts today. Modern society has only recently awakened to the perils we are storing up for ourselves in plundering the environment. Here is a prophet alerting his hearers to this many centuries ago.

God's Values

IN THESE ANCIENT words of Habakkuk we come close to the heart of the gospel with its concern for the disadvantaged and the outcast, indeed for all those who cannot help themselves. God's ways are not ours, nor are his values those of the world. The gospel overturns the hierarchical structures of society, as the Magnificat proclaims:

He has brought down the powerful from their thrones,
and lifted up the lowly;
he has filled the hungry with good things,
and sent the rich away empty.

LUKE 1:52–53

PRAYER
Lord, grant to us seeing eyes and loving hearts, that we may never in
our prosperity ignore poverty and distress, but may care and share so
that others, too, may rejoice in your good gifts.

ILL-GOTTEN GAINS

HERE THE PROPHET'S attention seems to turn once again to the avarice of individuals rather than nations. In fact, his words have a remarkable similarity to Jeremiah's condemnation of King Jehoiakim. The two prophets were virtually contemporary, and it may indeed be that Habakkuk, too, had this hostile king in mind.

Jeremiah had said:

> *Woe to him who builds his house by unrighteousness,*
> *and his upper rooms by injustice;*
> *who makes his neighbors work for nothing,*
> *and does not give them their wages.*
>
> JEREMIAH 22:13

But Habakkuk's words are less specific than Jeremiah's and his condemnation is more widely applicable. This is a challenge to any, of whatever generation, who set their priorities on personal aggrandizement and strive for the status dependent on impressive possessions, selfishly seeking their own security at the expense of others. Yet, says the prophet, they shall not go unpunished. Their iniquity will be proclaimed from the housetops, we might say. Habakkuk more graphically pictures the very stones and woodwork of the house crying out to testify to the monstrous injustice of those whose affluence is built on the bloodshed and suffering of others. What a contrast to Jesus' words as he rode triumphantly into Jerusalem on his final journey to the cross! "If these were silent," he said of the excited crowd, "the stones would shout out" (Luke 19:40).

A strong concern with social justice runs through the pages of the Old Testament. It was not only prophets like Amos who told his hearers in no uncertain terms that worship without justice was mere empty ritual and unacceptable to God (Amos 5:21–24). The laws in Deuteronomy, too, emphasize concern for fellow humans and for their animals (Deuteronomy 22:1–4, 8).

Evil on a Grander Scale

WITH THE THIRD "woe" (vv. 12–14) the prophet condemns a yet more extensive evil—whole towns and cities founded on violence and fraud. As before, his thought moves to and fro between the guilt of individuals and that of nations, primarily here the Babylonians. Their evil, along with their wealth and influence, are on a grander scale than Jehoiakim's (he was, after all, ruler of a tiny country), but it is the same in kind. They are "brothers beneath the skin." But for Habakkuk, with his prophetic vision, the last word does not lie with earth's transient kingdoms, however grand. There is a glorious hope, a better future, the culmination of God's judgment on the nations, on their arrogance and futility: "The earth will be filled with the knowledge of the glory of the Lord, as the waters cover the sea" (v. 14). Here is a different perspective, a glorious world filled with the awareness of God's presence and of his good purposes. Isaiah, in his famous portrayal of the coming Messiah, familiar to us through our Christmas readings, expresses a similar, though not identical, hope (Isaiah 11:9). But Habakkuk's vision goes even beyond Isaiah's in his emphasis on "the *glory* of the Lord."

The Bible delights in contrasting pictures in the New Testament as well as in the Old. Against the horrific description of war, pestilence, and famine in Revelation 6 is the glory of chapter 7: "Salvation belongs to our God who is seated on the throne, and to the Lamb!" (Revelation 7:10)

FOR PRAISE
Hallelujah! For the Lord God omnipotent reigneth.

From Handel's *Messiah*, based on Revelation 19:6

PUNISHMENT TO FIT THE CRIME

HABAKKUK'S WORDS, YET again, are deliberately ambiguous in their intended reference, applicable both on the international scene to the rising Babylonian power and, at the conclusion of this section, within Israel's own society, to their king, Jehoiakim. We may be surprised, in our ecologically sensitive days, to discover the breadth of the Old Testament's concern, in what we are inclined to discount as "primitive" times—concern for Lebanon and its wild creatures, plundered by the Babylonians like the Assyrians before them. Alternatively, Habakkuk's accusation may be directed against the notorious extravagance of King Jehoiakim (609–598 B.C.), obsessed as he was by the desire for kingly magnificence. Habakkuk's words are not specific and it is difficult to be certain. But Jeremiah, another prophet of Jehoiakim's time, was scathing in his criticism of the king's spacious palace with its airy roof chambers paneled with cedar and painted with vermilion:

> *Though your cedar is so splendid,*
> *does that prove you a king?*
> JEREMIAH 22:15, REB

Shame Instead of Glory

THE BABYLONIANS' TREATMENT of Israel and other small neighboring nations arose out of their desire to make a display of sheer, unadulterated power, for this was the overall motivation that lay at the heart of their life. Habakkuk has already described power as "their god." But their glory, transient like all human power, will be turned to shame. The image the prophet uses first to depict the humiliation of this arrogant nation is that of unprotected nakedness, exposed to public view. In contrast to the Greeks, the Israelites were embarrassed by nakedness and regarded it as shameful. Only in the pristine innocence of the garden of Eden, before the act of disobedience, were "the man and his wife . . . both naked, and . . . not ashamed" (Genesis 2:25).

The Cup of God's Wrath

HABAKKUK HAS NOT finished with contemptuous words against arrogance and self-regarding complacency. He takes up the striking image of a drunken orgy, which is used several times in the Old Testament to portray the state of desperation and chaos that overtakes the doomed, whether nation or individual. Associated with it, not only in the prophets but in one of the psalms too (Psalm 75:8), is the image of the "cup of God's wrath," a figure of speech that doubtless reflects abuses in everyday life whereby one person intoxicated another in order to abuse and humiliate him. In our present society, beset as it is by the problems of drink and drugs, this is a no less pertinent metaphor.

The Cup of Salvation

HABAKKUK'S WORDS END here on a note of doom. But, thank God, the Old Testament speaks not only of God's cup of wrath, but of the "cup of salvation," symbolized for Christians by the cup that Jesus shared with his disciples at the Last Supper.

Read Psalm 116 and rejoice with the psalmist whose thanksgiving overflows:

I love the Lord, because he has heard
my voice and my supplications.
Because he inclined his ear to me,
therefore I will call on him as long as I live . . .
What shall I return to the Lord
for all his bounty to me?
I will lift up the cup of salvation
and call on the name of the Lord.
                    PSALM 116:1–2, 12–13

PRAYER
Lord, help us to celebrate your salvation and daily deliverance with such
overwhelming thankfulness that it overflows into testimony to others by
our words and our lives.

THE ULTIMATE FOLLY

HABAKKUK REACHES THE climax of his "woes" with a satirical attack on the folly of idol worship. An idol is nothing but a "teacher of lies," a means of delusion. By repeating the word "maker," he ridicules the self-deception of placing one's trust in what one's own hands have shaped, though it is but a piece of cast metal. With a striking alliteration the prophet describes it, not as a god *(elohim)*, but as *elilim illemim,* "an idol that cannot speak."

Now comes the fifth and final "woe" against those foolish enough to expect movement and action from wood and silent (or lifeless) stone. Costly and gorgeous an idol may be with its gold and silver plating, yet static and lifeless, for there is no breath in it. Why, then, address oneself to that which cannot respond? From the beginning of Genesis, with its story of the making of humankind from the clay of the ground, through Ezekiel's vision of dry bones clothed with skin and flesh and sinews, to Paul's sermon in Athens ("[God] the universal giver of life and breath—indeed of everything," Acts 17:25, REB), the Bible affirms that there is no life without the breath of God.

But the Lord . . .

THERE IS ANOTHER actor in the drama, a new factor in the situation. Habakkuk has no need to spell out the difference between the lifeless idols, product of human craftsmanship, and the living Lord. The contrast is complete. The Lord is not embodied in images, however costly, but worshiped in his holy temple with its dark, empty sanctuary, the Holy of Holies. This God is holy and awe-inspiring, the universal God. It is not the Lord who is silent, but the worshipers who are hushed in solemnity in his presence (the Hebrew word *has* echoes the sound of hushing). He is wholly other, distinct from his creation. And here he is in his temple, with the implication that he has come as judge of all the earth.

The audience of this passage is not identified. The subject matter concerns both Babylonians and native Israelites, for they, too, succumbed to the temptation to seek after a God whom they could see, whose nearness they could feel. But the Old Testament is adamant: God the creator cannot be represented by anything that he has made, save only by humankind, male and female, made in the image of God—even though the image has been marred, all too often hidden and forgotten. This is God's challenge to us: We feel no inclination to worship an image, yet insidiously we may allow other things, material objects, ambitions, even relationships, to usurp the place of God. We are his image, however, created for that purpose, to be his representatives in the world.

PRAYER

Lord, keep us from the insidious temptation to let anything else, however precious, take first place in our lives. We are yours by creation and by redemption; grant us the will to glorify you day by day.

ULTIMATE FAITH

HABAKKUK'S BOOK BEGAN with a prayer. It ends similarly. In fact, the whole of the final chapter is a prayer modeled on the pattern of the psalms. But whereas Habakkuk's first prayer was a complaint to God, this time the prophet rehearses God's great deeds in the past and, trusting in this unchangeable God, commits himself in utter confidence for the future.

Verses 1–2 are a model of brevity in prayer. Habakkuk looks back to the past, to things he has learned by hearsay, but his faith is firsthand and deeply personal, and his prayer is urgent. It is for the present moment, for God's intervention in mercy. It is a personal prayer, yet offered on behalf of the community. In this way the prophet continues to fulfill his role as intercessor, just as he did in the opening verses of chapter 1. Since then he has brought God's message to the people; now he acts as intermediary between the people and God.

The Prophet and Liturgical Worship

THE FACT THAT Habakkuk's prayer is in the form of a psalm reminds us that the whole of the book was probably closely associated with liturgical worship. His complaints and his messages, and now this proclamation of God's greatness, are all to be seen in the context of worship. Like the psalms and like our Christian hymns and songs today, this prayer is couched in nonspecific terms, in language appropriate for use in many different situations.

The term "Shigionoth" in the title is uncertain in meaning. It probably indicates the tune to which the psalm is to be sung or the mood of music suited to it. Psalms were a regular part of Israel's worship, sung either by an individual or by a choir, with musical accompaniment.

Right at the beginning of his prayer the prophet makes an implicit confession of faith. God is not the God of past memories only, a God of great renown of whose deeds he has heard. This God, Habakkuk affirms, despite all appearances to the contrary, is God of the present moment,

God of his and his people's present. The prophet does not diminish God into a deity to be manipulated by human beings, guaranteed to be on the side of his people. Habakkuk's God is an awesome God, yet at the same time he approaches him with the boldness of faith. Habakkuk knows that God is not one with whom to trifle. He knows of his wrath, not the emotion of petty anger but the revulsion of God's holiness against wrong and injustice; he knows, too, of God's mercy. For judgment is not God's last word; it is his pathway to transformation and salvation.

The Importance of Remembering

ISRAEL, IN ITS public worship and within the family, passed on from one generation to another the story of God's great saving acts. But hearsay is not enough; it is secondhand. It needs to be reinforced by present experience. "I have heard," says Habakkuk, "I stand in awe," and now he pleads, "In our own time revive your work." Habakkuk's phrase, "in the midst of the years" (v. 2, NEB), suggests the moment between the ending of one year and the beginning of the next, celebrated in the great autumn harvest festival known as the Feast of Tabernacles, or Booths. Living in temporary shelters during the festival, the Israelites remembered how God led them through the desert into a land of freedom, so Habakkuk prays that now, too, they will experience his saving presence.

PRAYER

Lord, help us to look back and remember what you have done for us in the past, and then to go on in faith to meet each new day with eyes open to see your presence with us.

THE GLORY OF THE INVISIBLE GOD

HABAKKUK'S POETRY THRILLS our hearts with this awesome picture of God in his glorious splendor. This is no mere superman, a human being writ large, a deity to be manipulated, but God whose glory fills all things, all space, both heaven and earth. God is invisible and indescribable; he is beyond all human thought. No image can ever represent him. The nearest the prophet-poet can come to describing God's glory is the brilliant blazing sun, and perhaps the dazzling lightning ("rays came forth from his hand"). But God's power is controlled, hidden in his hand until he chooses to unleash it.

The Desert God

IT IS INTERESTING that God is not described as coming from Jerusalem but, in accordance with Israel's more ancient traditions, from the southern desert. Teman and Mount Paran were areas through which Israel had traveled on its desert journey from Egypt to Mount Sinai under Moses' leadership. The Lord is a God of movement, not static, nor tied to a particular location, but journeying with his people. The link with the south may also represent the practical experience of life in Israel; the sirocco blowing from the southern desert heralded the season's welcome change and the approach of the life-giving autumn rains.

Selah

THE SIGNIFICANCE OF this notation, which occurs twice in Habakkuk's prayer and frequently in the psalms, is unclear. It may be a musical notation urging the instrumentalists to lift up their music, or a direction to the singers to hymn a doxology giving glory to God, for here is God's triumph over the powerful forces of nature. He is not a God to be trifled with, but is sovereign in his majesty.

Glimpses of Glory

THE MEANING OF the allusion to pestilence and plague is uncertain. These were two Canaanite gods, Deber (Pestilence) and Resheph (Plague), whose defeat by the god Baal was celebrated in Canaanite poetry. It may be that the prophet visualizes them as attendant on Yahweh and under his control, just as the fierce sun of the Middle East is both life-giving and destructive in its power. Another suggestion visualizes these malevolent deities scattering as God approaches, like small animals that scatter before a human tread. Even the everlasting hills and mountains shake before the approach of this mighty God, and the black bedouin tents of the southern desert tremble, as the prophet had seen them torn by the powerful wind. Neither nature nor humankind is untouched by his majestic coming. Yet, as elsewhere throughout the Old Testament, God himself is unseen; there are only glimpses of his glory.

The Gospels, too, speak of God's glory. In the Synoptics (Matthew, Mark, and Luke) the glory with which Christ is invested at the transfiguration is an overwhelming external radiance, visible to the disciples. In John's Gospel, "glory" takes on a different, subtler meaning. God's glory is manifested supremely in the cross, not as an external radiance visible to physical sight, but through the self-giving of the world's Savior in suffering, humiliation, and death.

FOR MEDITATION

Declare his glory among the nations,
his marvelous works among all the peoples.
For great is the Lord, and greatly to be praised;
he is to be revered above all gods.
For all the gods of the peoples are idols,
but the Lord made the heavens.

PSALM 96:3–5

THE CREATOR'S VICTORY OVER CHAOS

HABAKKUK IS A visionary, and his poetic language in these verses is apt
to bewilder us unless we realize that what he is describing here is God's
creative activity, portrayed as a battle against the forces of Chaos. For
poetic representations like Habakkuk's we have to look, not at the familiar
creation stories in Genesis 1 and 2, but at the psalms. A glance at Psalm
89:9–14 will illustrate the range of ideas on which Habakkuk is drawing.
There God is depicted as defeating the Chaos monster, Rahab ("the arrogant one," see page 10), and scattering his enemies with his mighty arm.
But it is clear from the context that the psalmist is thinking of creation,
and in his use of the words "rule" and "throne" he is acclaiming God as
the universal king-creator who keeps in check all the forces of chaos. It
comes as no surprise that the setting of this psalm is the great autumn
festival at which Israel acclaimed God as both Creator and king, giving
thanks for harvest past and praying for fertile rain for harvest to come.

Habakkuk's Picture Language

ANCIENT ISRAEL WAS not a seagoing people, unlike the Philistine nation.
For Israel, the sea and the raging wadis were a terrifying force, a symbol of
the primeval waters of Chaos, which God had subdued in creation when he
divided the waters and caused the dry land to appear. The language used
here of storm and torrent, of flashing lightning and crashing waves, is
drawn from the fierce storms and the flash floods that are experienced from
time to time in Canaan, even in the desert. But the prophet has no intention of confusing God with the forces of nature. As Creator, he is wholly
other than his creation. Yet to speak meaningfully of the power of God,
whom they could not see, ancient Israel's psalmists drew by analogy on
the mightiest of the forces that they could see—the great storms, devastating in their magnificence, that swept their land.

The pictures are vivid. Even the sun and moon feel the awesome presence as God drives his chariot over the desert with speeding arrows and

flashing spear. And in verse 12 Habakkuk turns from nature to history, from the chaos of nature to that of human hostility. Yet through it all, the purpose of his coming is made clear: He comes in salvation to deliver his people and their anointed king, forerunner of the Messiah and the agent of God's rule on earth. The military language may not be attractive to us today, but brutal warfare was, and is, a reality in the world. Judah was faced with a life-threatening crisis. The fall of Jerusalem and the destruction of the temple were imminent. It is in the face of this that Habakkuk celebrates the power of God to save. The oppressors who "open their jaws to devour their wretched victims in secret" (v. 14, REB) must be defeated if the helpless are to be rescued. Here is the prophet's confident answer to his earlier complaints against God. Despite everything, despite the anxiety and the patient waiting, God *is* coming to deliver his people from all that would harm them.

FOR MEDITATION
Israel's prophets were realists. They faced the present realities of an unjust world, yet committed the future to the God of justice. May we, too, share that faith.

The Lord saw it and it displeased him
that there was no justice.
He saw that there was no one,
and was appalled that there was no one to intervene;
so his own arm brought him victory,
and his righteousness upheld him.
ISAIAH 59:15B–16

FROM FEAR TO FAITH

THE EXTREMES OF emotion expressed in these last verses are striking. Habakkuk's vision has a profound effect on him physically. First the prophet succumbs to weakness and fear as he awaits the calamity that will fall on his enemies. For God's advent in judgment is an overwhelming experience to the oppressed as well as to the oppressor, even though for Habakkuk and his people it is the harbinger of salvation. God is not to be trifled with. He is awesome both in judgment and in salvation, as the writer of the epistle to the Hebrews recognized: "Let us . . . offer to God an acceptable worship with reverence and awe; for indeed our God is a consuming fire" (Hebrews 12:28–29).

Yet fear changes to faith. Was it because of his quiet waiting for God to intervene (v. 16)? Then the prophet breaks into a supreme expression of confidence. Prayers and hopes at the autumn festival focused on the needs of the coming year for the early and the latter rain to secure the life-giving harvest. But the prophet feels so strongly the overwhelming joy of God's presence that he affirms, even if all else shall fail, even if there shall be no harvest to support life—failure in all of nature's provision—yet, "I will rejoice in the Lord; I will exult in the God of my salvation."

The Lord's Presence, the Greatest of His Gifts

HABAKKUK HAS LEARNED that trust in God is not dependent on his outward gifts, the signs of his blessing. Ultimately it is God himself, his unseen presence, even if all outward evidence of his blessing is absent, that is totally satisfying. Nor is Habakkuk's a grudging, self-abasing reliance on God when devoid of all his gifts. This is the life-giving God, the God who imparts strength and joy. And Habakkuk's book, which opened with a querulous complaint against God, concludes with the delightful picture of a deer on the mountainsides, liberated, energized, and effortless. Such is the transformation that can take place, not after deliverance from troubles and affliction, but within them, when God's presence becomes the one prize above all others—for his God, the one whom he worships and to whom he has committed himself for life or for death, is *the Lord.*

Habakkuk and the Psalms

WE HAVE NOTED several links between Habakkuk's prayer and the psalms. Like everyone in ancient Israel, Habakkuk was familiar with the psalms through their use in worship. Scholars have little doubt that Habakkuk's own prayer, with its powerful poetry and dramatic portrayal of God, was intended for liturgical use in worship. Habakkuk's own joyful affirmation of faith independent of circumstances is close to the psalmist's total commitment to God in the famous words of Psalm 73:25–26:

Whom have I in heaven but you?
And there is nothing on earth that I desire other than you.
My flesh and my heart may fail,
but God is the strength of my heart and my portion forever.

The concluding words of the book closely resemble elements in some of the psalm titles (Psalms 4 and 6), giving a clear indication of the continued use of Habakkuk's words in worship. His prayer is indeed a psalm outside the psalter.

PRAYER
"Although . . . yet . . ."

Lord, make me so aware of your very self, that I may value your presence above all your gifts and share Habakkuk's confidence, that with God all shall be well.

CALLED TO ACCOUNT

THE BOOK OF Zephaniah starts, as most books do, with a title that tells us who the author is and what its content is.

The Author

THE AUTHOR IS "the LORD," written in our English Bibles in capital letters to remind us that this is the solemn divine name YHWH, often pronounced Yahweh, although no one is exactly certain how it was pronounced originally. The Hebrew alphabet is very different from the English one in that it consists entirely of consonants. Printed Hebrew Bibles include vowel points (dots and other signs added mostly above and below the letters) in order to clarify and to safeguard the meaning of the scriptures, but by the time this system was in use, the divine name had long been regarded as too holy to be uttered. So the vowel points traditionally added to the name YHWH throughout the Old Testament are those belonging to the word *Adonai,* which means "the Lord," and indicate that this word is to be read in place of the sacred name. If this customary practice is misunderstood and YHWH is read with the vowels of *Adonai,* the result is the name Jehovah.

The content of the book is "the word of the LORD that came. . . ." It comes to God's people through a prophet and it is their responsibility to listen, but it has *already come* to the prophet and he has had to listen. The prophets were conscious that the message they were commissioned to give was backed by an authority greater than their own. It was God's message, and often it was a difficult, uncongenial message to give. They were, after all, usually addressing their own people.

The Lord's Messenger

THE IDENTITY OF the messenger is important. The Lord chose his messengers with care. The prophet's personality mattered, and so did his circumstances and experiences. They had made him what he was. And to be a prophet was a costly ministry, often painful, sometimes dangerous. Unlike the telephone, an impersonal instrument that merely transmits a message from one individual to another, the prophet as God's messenger was deeply involved with the message. God chose the right person for the right time to carry his message, and he still does. The messages of the prophets are not a homogeneous collection indistinguishable from each other; they come from specific prophets to meet the needs of particular times.

It looks as though Zephaniah may have had an African ancestor; Cush was the name for Ethiopia, and Cushi may well have come from that country. Whether his great-great-grandfather, Hezekiah, was the king of that name is uncertain. The period of Zephaniah's ministry coincided with the reign of Josiah (640–609 B.C.). Josiah is renowned for his religious reforms, in which he set out to abolish practices unworthy of the Lord's worship. You can read this story in 2 Kings 22–23. The scroll that was discovered in the Jerusalem temple during the course of Josiah's reforms is generally regarded as the central section of the book of Deuteronomy (chapters 12–26). The nature of Zephaniah's denunciations that follow suggests that he was preaching his message somewhat before Josiah's reforms, probably about 630 B.C.

PRAYER

Lord, you know my personality, my circumstances, and the variety of my experiences in life. I pray that in your own way and in your own time, you will use me to serve your purpose in the world.

GOD SWEEPS CLEAN

ZEPHANIAH IS A poet and his words are hard-hitting:

I will sweep the earth clean of all that is on it, says the Lord.
I will sweep away both man and beast,
I will sweep the birds from the air and the fish from the sea (NEB).

Blunt, shocking words! Some English translations set out Zephaniah's message as poetry, and this is a help. It reminds us as we read that this is not a coldly logical statement. Poetry uses images, creating powerful pictures that flash on our minds and startle us. It aims to challenge and involve us.

The Reversal of Creation

THIS THREEFOLD REPETITION of "sweep" (found in several English translations), in which we almost hear the swish of a broom, is closer to the sound of the two Hebrew words *asoph aseph* ("to gather up" and "destroy") than the less colorful though certainly accurate "I shall utterly destroy . . ." of the Revised English Bible. Zephaniah is a poet, and the words *asoph aseph* are skillfully chosen to suit the occasion of his message, the Feast of Ingathering *(Asiph)*. This was the last of the three annual pilgrim festivals in ancient Israel. You will find it mentioned in Exodus 23:16. This was the great autumn festival, often known as the Feast of Tabernacles, or Booths, the final harvest thanksgiving of the year, when God was celebrated as king and Creator. It is not for nothing, then, that the picture of judgment is seen as a reversal of God's creative activity in Genesis 1.

Preparing for Salvation

WHAT ARE WE to make of a passage like this? Is this the vengeful God of the Old Testament, according to popular thought, who has little to do with the loving God of the New Testament? That would be a superficial attitude to our passage. We shall find as we read on in Zephaniah that when God sweeps clean, he is getting ready for a new start, a fresh beginning. His judgment is preparing the way for salvation. And Zephaniah sets out to startle his hearers in order to make them listen and mend their ways. Imagine the scene: crowds of worshipers from distant villages come to Jerusalem to celebrate the festival, a noisy, joyful gathering, rejoicing at the harvest gathered in and looking forward to next season's blessing. And suddenly the atmosphere of celebration is shattered. Here is a prophet with disagreeable words of doom. There's no room now for complacency. Zephaniah's first hearers wouldn't miss the powerful play on words: this may be *Asiph* ("Ingathering"), but God is going to "sweep clean" *(asoph aseph)*.

Why This Message?

ZEPHANIAH IS CONCERNED about what it means to worship God—the real, living, holy God, not a God who is merely humanity writ large, a superman. Having a right view of God means having a right view of ourselves. We are free to choose, but we are accountable for our choices. We cannot sin with impunity. God has the last word.

PRAYER

Loving Lord, we confess our complacency and self-satisfaction. Grant that we may not be weighed down by guilt but, liberated by your forgiveness, may live in faith and hope.

"NO OTHER GODS BESIDE ME"

THE BROAD SWEEP of the previous verses is left behind. The focus narrows to Zephaniah's own audience, the people of Judah and Jerusalem. It is one thing to listen to denunciation of other people's shortcomings, quite another when it hits home. You, the worshipers at the festival, says Zephaniah, are the guilty ones. Purporting to worship Yahweh the creator, they had broken his first commandment: "Have no other gods beside me" (Exodus 20:3). All sorts of idolatrous practices were taking place right there in Jerusalem. Some were worshiping the Canaanite god Baal; others had turned to astral deities ("the host of heaven"). And some were hedging their bets, claiming allegiance to Yahweh but making sure that if he failed them, they had Milcom, an Ammonite god, to call on. All these were the kinds of worship Josiah was soon to root out as unworthy of the Lord Almighty (2 Kings 23:13). And then there were some who made no pretense to worship at all; they were atheists in practice who simply ignored the Lord, living their lives as if God did not exist.

The Day of the Lord

REMEMBER, THE OCCASION was a sacred festival, and here in verse 7 is its climax, the hushed silence celebrating God's awesome coming among the worshipers. Notice the impressive title Zephaniah gives him, this God on whom many of his so-called worshipers have turned their backs. He is the Lord GOD, and this time it is GOD in capital letters that represents the divine name YHWH. Yes, agrees Zephaniah, the Lord Yahweh *is* coming among us, but his presence will mean judgment, not blessing. The prophet's words are ominous and full of bitter irony. In a daring image, too horrific to make explicit, the prophet pictures the Lord himself preparing to offer sacrifice; the invited guests, leaders, and people of Judah are themselves the victims.

What is it to which Zephaniah so strongly objects? Foreign fashions and dancing on the temple terrace, or leaping over the temple threshold (the meaning is not clear), sound harmless enough. After all, the psalms are exuberant with music and dancing in worship. But these practices were more sinister than they at first appear, and it was their implications that troubled the prophet. Foreign fashions signified an absorption into foreign culture and religion, probably here a result of assimilating the ways of their Assyrian overlords, a pagan, oppressive nation. The result inevitably was the loss of national identity as the people of God and their witness in the world. Dancing on the terrace of the temple, or leaping over the threshold, symbolized acknowledgment of other deities and a resurgence of superstition, the fear of spirits from which recognition of God's kingship frees us. But, however obscure and antiquated are the practices to which Zephaniah refers, their outcome is unmistakable—crimes of violence and deception. Here is a challenge for us today when confronted with what may seem to be harmless practices. It is not the action itself, but its implications, of which we need to be aware in making our choices.

PRAYER

Sovereign Lord, our creator and our king, your worship is no easy option but costly and demanding. Help us to trust you fully, and so to find your way for us which is life and freedom.

THE FUTILITY OF MATERIALISM

THERE IS AN urgency about Zephaniah's message; God's day of judgment is at hand. It is not only the top people in the community, the leaders and officials, who are to be blamed for the disintegration of society. The rot has set in throughout. Now the prophet turns his spotlight onto the business class, the merchants. In the absence of minted coins they are busily weighing out silver for their trading. There is no specific accusation here of dishonesty. Rather, the fault lies in their total absorption with their moneymaking, with no time left for God.

A More Ominous Din

IMAGINE THE NOISY markets, the shouts of the hawkers and the haggling of the traders. That din and bustle will be replaced by a far more ominous sound, says the prophet, "a cry . . . a wail . . . a loud crash," right at the heart of their commerce. Zephaniah's words are startling, demanding attention. He names the familiar areas of Jerusalem's commercial district, the Fish Gate, close to the Sheep Gate, where years later Jesus healed a sick man (John 5:2–9), the Second Quarter and the lower town, the site perhaps of Jerusalem's main market, known as the Mortar, from its resemblance in shape to mortars used for crushing wheat. He makes no criticism of trade itself; the trouble was materialism, which left no room in life for spiritual values, only for the hard sell, the ruthless greed.

The All-seeing God

THEN THERE WERE the sleek and prosperous, the comfortable middle class, grown apathetic. The prophets used down-to-earth language, pictures taken from everyday life, to illustrate their message, just as Jesus did. God is pictured here searching out the dark corners of the city with his lamp, in much the same way as the woman in Jesus' parable was searching for her lost coin (Luke 15:8). Lighting was not as good in those days as in our brightly lit cities and homes, where the dark corners can be quickly illuminated. It was a slower, more painstaking business then. But God is thorough, says Zephaniah, and there is no escape for the sinful.

The target of the prophet's warning this time is the comfortably complacent, stagnating over their wine, or perhaps Zephaniah is likening them to wine thickening or congealing because it has been left too long and has passed its shelf life. As far as they are concerned, they believe in God. Oh, yes, he exists; of that they have no doubt. But their beliefs and actions don't match up, and as far as their lives are concerned, God isn't involved at all. He is inactive and unconcerned, a remote, uncaring deity. Real commitment to God in loyal love was no easier then than now. Times change, but human nature doesn't. All their wealth, whether possessions, houses, or vineyards, will let them down as ultimate security. They needed to be reminded of what the psalmist knew:

Unless the Lord builds the house,
those who build it labor in vain.
PSALM 127:1

PRAYER

Lord, help me in all my busy working life to remember that you are the "everyday God," concerned with everything I do. Grant that each day I may live out in my life what I believe in my heart and bear witness to your holy presence.

NO TIME TO LOSE

THE BOOK OF Zephaniah began with God calling his people to account. Here now is the reckoning, the final balance sheet. The responsibility is theirs. They have made their choice, just as we must make ours, for or against God—and the result is joy or disaster.

. . . and the End Is Death

THESE LAST, POWERFUL verses of chapter 1 paint a horrific picture of the devastation and brutality of war. This is poetry, in effect a battle song, and the warrior pictured here is the Lord. As in all poetry, the language is not literal but symbolic. Sight and sound, darkness and cloud, trumpet blast and battle cry, conjure up a scene of doom and death in terms familiar to the ancient world, where brutality was an everyday occurrence. Sadly, such horrors still happen. To us they are no less familiar. We shrink from such a picture of God, but we cannot shrink from the seriousness of sin. Putting wealth in place of God, rejecting his life-giving love, doesn't always bring obvious physical disaster, as the Old Testament writers knew very well, but it always brings spiritual disaster.

God Has No Favorites

THE "GREAT DAY of the Lord," celebrated in Israel's autumn festival, will be, by their own choice, a time of doom, not of blessing. God is not a useful ally to be taken up or neglected at will and for one's own convenience. He is the Lord, the judge, of all the earth. He has no favorites. And so in the midst of their comfortable and heedless celebrations, Zephaniah turns the familiar and comforting into the challenging and disturbing. This was the commission of the prophets, as it was of Jesus.

All these harsh words are words of warning. The prophet longs to lead his people back to God, the source of all blessing. Words of encouragement follow in chapter 2. God doesn't delight in death. He is the living, loving Lord, and in the end this same prophet will tell of evil removed, of transformation, of joy and singing.

The Old Testament, like the New Testament, is full of God's love and forgiveness and both Testaments alike emphasize the seriousness of trifling with God, not just the folly but the catastrophe of turning one's back on the living Lord. But in the New Testament there is this immense difference, that God's judgment has been suffered already by one who willingly took the place of sinners, the innocent for the guilty. "With his stripes we are healed" (Isaiah 53:5, RSV).

MEDITATION

Reread this passage, then turn to John 3:16–17 and rejoice in the fullness of the gospel message:

God so loved the world that he gave his only Son, so that everyone who believes in him may not perish but may have eternal life. Indeed, God did not send the Son into the world to condemn the world, but in order that the world might be saved through him.

Our fitting response is surely that of the great apostle Paul: "Thanks be to God for his indescribable gift!"

2 CORINTHIANS 9:15

PRIDE HUMILIATED

A Glimmer of Hope

CHAPTER 1 WAS dark and full of foreboding; its message was God's judgment on sin. Yet, harsh and distressing though the prophet's words sounded, they were born out of compassion, the will to work a transformation, to avoid disaster. And so at last in chapter 2 we find a glimmer of hope. Yet, for all that, it is a somber chapter describing in vivid picture-language God's victory over everything that stands in opposition to his kingdom. The prophet speaks first to Jerusalem, then he reaches out to the four points of the compass, for God is the universal king. Nowhere is beyond his concern and control.

A Warning

THE WORDS SOUND harsh, but they are a warning to Jerusalem to take action before it is too late. The "day of the Lord," foreshadowed in the yearly joyful celebration of God at the great autumn Feast of Tabernacles, or Booths, becomes, in the light of the world's sin, not a day of rejoicing but "the day of the Lord's anger" (vv. 2–3). The poetry is impressive. It compels attention. The five lines of verses 2–3 all begin in Hebrew with the letter *b*, creating the impression of a solemn drumbeat, difficult though it is to recreate this adequately in English:

> *before (beterem) . . . before (beterem) . . . before (beterem) . . .*
> *seek (baqqeshu) . . . seek (baqqeshu) . . .*

These are solemn words of warning, yet warning always implies hope, the opportunity for a better future. There still *is* time, says the prophet, for the nation to take stock. There is a moment's respite before the judgment; there is a way to return to the Lord. But complacency will not do. It needs decisive action and the will to choose the right. "Seek the Lord . . . seek righteousness, seek humility," the prophet begs his audience, but he adds a "perhaps." God is not at human disposal. He is the supreme Lord, and repentance is not a kind of magic charm. Escape from disaster is not automatic, a foregone conclusion. Yet God does not ignore those who come in humility and obedience. Notice how these two belong together. When we think about it, they are the negative and positive poles of repentance; humility acknowledges the seriousness of sin and obedience means resolving to turn in a new direction.

Deliverance for All

SALVATION IN THE Old Testament is often, though by no means always, pictured in terms of deliverance from war and invasion. Israel then, as now, was a small nation, its precarious existence often threatened by the military powers of the day. Salvation for Israel meant defeat for its enemies. In the New Testament salvation is described in very different terms. It is personal, not national; spiritual, not material. Christ's victory means defeat of evil, and all, of whatever race, can share his triumph.

PRAYER

Lord, grant us the will to make a new beginning and to follow henceforward in the steps of him who is the way, the truth, and the life.

THE LORD CONDEMNS ARROGANCE

THE PROPHET'S VISION is not restricted to Jerusalem. His God is Lord of all the earth. The psalms, too, make this clear in their summons to all nations to worship him, the universal king. God's message through the prophet is targeted on the four points of the compass, first the Philistine cities on Israel's western border, then Moab and Ammon to the east, and finally, by the end of this chapter, Ethiopia to the south and Assyria to the north.

The Philistines

THE PHILISTINES WERE renowned as a seagoing, warlike people. In biblical tradition their most famous warrior had been Goliath, whose scornful defiance of "the armies of the living God" had been confounded by David, an unknown youth with an unsophisticated weapon, a sling and five pebbles. This famous story is found in 1 Samuel 17. The Philistines originated in the Mediterranean area and later expanded eastward, settling around 1200 B.C. in the coastal areas of Palestine, in what we know today as the Gaza strip and the territory to its north and east.

The prophet doesn't waste time on vague generalities; his language is down-to-earth and specific. First he names the four great Philistine cities—Gaza, Ashkelon, Ashdod, and Ekron—Israel's near neighbors. The fifth Philistine city, Gath, from which Goliath came, had by this time declined in importance. Danger is near, Zephaniah warns—and unexpected. This seems to be the significance of his reference to "noon" (v. 4), the heat of the day when attack was least expected. The prophets were poets and often they gave an added edge to their message by playing on the sound of the words. So here "Gaza" *('azza)* resembles the word "deserted" *('azuba)* and Ekron *('eqron)* sounds like the word for "uprooted" *(te'aqer)*.

A Demanding Faith

WHEN THE PROPHETS pronounced judgment like this on other nations, as they often did, they were not simply being chauvinistic. It was not that their own nation could count on privileged protection, as though God would inevitably side with Israel. The prophets protest against such a narrowly nationalistic complacency as a diminution of the almighty and sovereign Lord. That is why it is important to remember that Israel, too, comes under God's judgment, and is the first to be challenged by the prophets to repent. Commitment to Yahweh was no cozy option. It was as demanding and life-transforming then as it is now, and often Israel was tempted to choose an easier way.

Moabites and Ammonites

NEXT ZEPHANIAH TURNS his attention to the Moabites and Ammonites. Moab lay to the east of the Dead Sea, an agricultural and pastoral land enriched with splendid buildings and defended along its borders by fortresses. There was a long history of hostility between Moab and Israel. On the famous Moabite stone of the ninth century B.C., Mesha, king of Moab, proudly claimed that he had destroyed Israel forever.

Ammon lay east of the Jordan, to the north of Moab. The Ammonites' relationship with Israel had fluctuated over the centuries, friendly at times, more often hostile. Both nations, says Zephaniah, had been guilty of the same scornful attitude as Goliath was; "they scoffed and boasted against the people of the Lord of hosts" (v. 10). Against them God will assert his kingly rule, in salvation for those who trust him, in judgment for those who oppose him. Remember that these words are poetry; they are symbolic rather than literal. Remember, too, their context. Israel was a small nation struggling for existence in a hostile world; for them deliverance meant defeat of their enemies. Our deliverance, too, has meant death, not this time the death of enemies but the death of the Savior.

PRAYER

Lord, grant that we may never treat lightly your forgiveness, but always remember what it cost you to bring us life.

THE DOWNFALL OF PRIDE

THE ETHIOPIANS TO the south, in the area stretching down from Aswan to the junction with the Nile near modern Khartoum, are passed over quickly and the prophet immediately focuses attention on the north, the direction from which the most pressing danger threatened. Israel's prime enemy at this time was Assyria, a powerful and ruthless foe. The book of Nahum gives evidence of that aggressive nation's notorious brutality, from which Israel had suffered over many years. The reversal of Assyria's fortunes that Zephaniah depicts is dramatic. It is grounded in his confidence that no human might, however great, can withstand the Lord.

Nineveh, the last capital of Assyria, was renowned in the ancient world for its splendid architecture and its massive defenses. It was there that some of the great Assyrian rulers, such as Sennacherib in Isaiah's time, had their palaces. A relief carving of a lion hunt from about 640 B.C., which had adorned the palace of Ashurbanipal, the Assyrian king who reigned from 668 to 627 and whose later years thus coincided with the ministry of Zephaniah, can be seen in the British Museum. Nineveh fell before the rising Babylonian power in August of the year 612 B.C., as Nahum and Zephaniah had predicted. Little more than two decades had passed since Zephaniah's words were spoken. His portrayal of Nineveh's ruin creates a desolate scene with the eerie sounds of owls hooting and ravens cawing, populated only by herds and wild animals. Even now the ruins of Nineveh's citadel are known as the "Mound of many sheep." Its description as "a dry waste like the desert" (v. 13) is particularly ironic since Nineveh was famous for its canal structure, which maintained plentiful supplies of water within the city.

Lament over Nineveh

THE FINAL VERSE is in the style of a lament and is heavy with irony. It recounts not the virtues and renown of the fallen city, but its vices, above all its pride and its arrogant isolation. All this flaunted pride has ended in desolation. Nineveh, says Zephaniah, will be an object of scorn, mocked by passersby with hissing and shaking of the fist, gestures of extreme horror still seen among Palestinian Arabs.

Throughout this chapter a key theme has been the perils of pride. Israel was urged to seek humility. Moab and Ammon were condemned for their pride "because they scoffed and boasted against the people of the Lord of hosts" (v. 10). And now Nineveh's pride, too, is to end in disaster—a city so exultant and secure, so self-satisfied and complacent that it had little thought beyond its own prosperity and fame: "I am, and there is no one else" (v. 15).

The Sin of Pride

THIS IS A RECURRENT theme in the Old Testament—the condemnation of arrogant superiority that ignores human limitations and usurps the place of God, denying his sovereignty over human affairs. Zephaniah's incisive description of Nineveh's proud isolation reminds us of Ezekiel's powerful portrayal of Egypt's self-confident pharaoh: "My Nile is my own: I made it . . ." (Ezekiel 29:3).

The temptation to pride is part of the human condition. The early Christian church was not exempt, and nor are we. The apostle Paul had to warn the Christians in Philippi, "Do nothing from selfish ambition or conceit, but in humility regard others as better than yourselves" (Philippians 2:3).

PRAYER

Lord, guard us from the temptation to pride and self-satisfaction. In your mercy keep us humble, make us holy, and fill us with your Spirit.

THE FOLLY OF IGNORING GOD

JUDGMENT HAS COME full circle. From the nations around, west, east, south, and north, the prophet targets his own people. Israel itself falls under God's judgment. The condemnation is uninhibited. He describes the nation as "tyrant, filthy, foul" (v. 1, REB). And its sin? The obduracy which meant it "listened to no voice," not even God's; it refused correction, and didn't trust the Lord or draw near to him in devotion.

The leaders, all of them, civil and religious alike, are guilty. This is poetry, and each line of verses 3–4 begins dramatically by specifying the target of its accusation: officials, judges, prophets, priests. The civic leaders are avaricious, the religious leaders reckless in their disregard of their God-given task. In short, they have acted as if there were no God to whom they must one day render account. The first word of verse 5 breaks the sequence. There is another to be reckoned with—Yahweh, the Lord, and he is just, utterly dependable, day in and day out.

The Compassion in God's Heart

IN PRACTICAL TERMS justice for the oppressed means judgment on the oppressor, in this case not a foreign nation but Jerusalem itself, a city where people were suffering. They had seen God's activity in history among the nations, and yet Jerusalem, God's holy city, had plunged on heedlessly, eager in the pursuit of wickedness. (The Hebrew of verse 7 conjures up a vivid picture: "They got up betimes to corrupt all their actions.") Here is a poignant picture of the Lord yearning in affection over his people. The Good News Bible with its simple, colloquial language captures the emotion in the heart of God: "I thought that my people would have reverence for me and accept my discipline, that they would never forget the lesson I taught them. But soon they were behaving as badly as ever."

Sometimes we think of God as an impassive deity. The Old Testament, like the New Testament, reveals the vulnerability of God, his sorrow that springs from love rejected, for love by its very nature is vulnerable. These words in Zephaniah are not far removed in intent from Jesus' sorrowful longing for his people: "Jerusalem, Jerusalem . . . How often have I desired to gather your children together as a hen gathers her brood under her wings, and you were not willing!" (Matthew 23:37) Here as elsewhere we notice echoes of the Old Testament in the Gospels.

MEDITATION AND PRAYER

Read meditatively Hosea 11:1–4 and 8–9 and reflect on God, the loving parent, teaching his child to walk and gently tending its bruises:

> *It was I who taught Ephraim to walk,*
> *I who took them in my arms;*
> *but they did not know that I secured them with reins*
> *and led them with bonds of love,*
> *that I lifted them like a little child to my cheek,*
> *that I bent down to feed them.*
>
> HOSEA 11:3–4, REB

God of love, grant that we may learn what love truly is and follow daily in the steps of divine Love crucified for us.

JUDGMENT REVERSED

"THEREFORE WAIT FOR me," says the Lord. The words are chilling in this context. Generally they refer to waiting for God's salvation:

Our soul waits for the Lord;
he is our help and our shield.
      PSALM 33:20

But here in Zephaniah they are used in bitter irony. God as king and judge rises from his throne to pronounce sentence. This is not a vindictive God acting out of petty jealousy. He is the Lord of all nations, creator of all the earth, and savior to whom uncompromising allegiance is due. That is why the first of the Ten Commandments is this: "You must have no other god beside me" (Exodus 20:2, REB).

A New Unity

YET, IF GOD is truly to be God, sin can never have the last word. With one of those sudden, unexpected changes of tone found elsewhere in the prophets, judgment becomes salvation. God takes the initiative; hope lies not in human reformation but in divine transformation. Here is a reversal of the Tower of Babel story (Genesis 11). All the earth had one common language, but the people's arrogance overreached itself. The Lord confused their language and scattered them. Their pristine unity was lost. But now Zephaniah, portraying a future of hope, tells of a new unity, another language. The echoes are deliberate. In place of confused speech will be pure, unadulterated speech; instead of making a name for themselves they will call on the Lord's name, serving him "shoulder to shoulder" (v. 9; the Hebrew is literally, "with one shoulder"); instead of scattering there will be gathering of the peoples. A glance back to the ancient Genesis story emphasizes the power that people have when they act in unison; "nothing that they propose to do will now be impossible for them," says God (Genesis 11:6). We can transpose those words to Zephaniah's picture of the future—with God's renewal nothing will be impossible. Paul, the great apostle, was heartened in this confidence: "I can do all things through him who strengthens me" (Philippians 4:13).

Here in Zephaniah, God offers his people forgiveness. Even the sense of shame for their past rebellion will be obliterated. But this transformation has its cost; self-pride must be abandoned: "You shall no longer be haughty in my holy mountain" (v. 11).

Here is the ideal, which runs like a continuous thread through the Hebrew scriptures, of true humility that refuses to act in complacent independence and draws its strength from the Lord. Then, in the great future day when God takes action, says Zephaniah, there will be freedom from wrong and with it freedom from fear.

MEDITATION AND PRAYER
Read prayerfully Psalm 57:1–3:

Be merciful to me, O God, be merciful to me,
for in you my soul takes refuge;
in the shadow of your wings I will take refuge,
until the destroying storms pass by.
I cry to God Most High,
to God who fulfills his purpose for me.
He will send from heaven and save me.

Lord, grant me that true humility that comes from acknowledging your majesty, might, and love. Lead me to trust you in life and in death, for you have loved me even to the point of death, a cruel death on a cross.

TWO JOYFUL SONGS

THE LAST VERSES of the book of Zephaniah are full of singing. Through suffering and disaster, God in his own time works deliverance. Here is the counterbalance to the words of doom with which the book began. There was little point for a prophet to proclaim doom to the nation if that was God's final word, without the possibility of hope beyond. This is the presumption of the whole Old Testament since the expulsion of Adam and Eve from the Garden of Eden—that God transforms disaster into salvation.

The First Song

AS IN THE psalms of praise (for example Psalm 95), God's people are summoned to exuberant song; they are called to praise his triumphs: "sing aloud . . . shout . . . rejoice and exult." There was nothing restrained or inhibited about Israel's worship. It was a noisy, exuberant affair with music and dancing. And the cause of celebration here in verses 14–17 is that "the king of Israel, the Lord, is in your midst." The great autumn Festival of Tabernacles with which Zephaniah's opening words were associated, in addition to thanksgiving for harvest past and prayers for the harvest to come, included celebration of Yahweh's kingship. It is in this context that Zephaniah's song of praise belongs. God is a God of reversals, a God of transformation beyond any human power of reformation. When all hope seems gone, there is hope in God. And here we find the first, and only, mention of God's love in Zephaniah. It is this love that brings renewal to his people and gives victory over all that would destroy them. But they have a part to play too. It is for them to respond in trust. No wonder it is not only the human worshipers who are called upon to join in song. God himself rejoices over them, singing loudly in his triumph.

The Second Song

AND HERE, IN verses 18–20, is God's song, a promise of blessing to those he has delivered. It is not by chance that there is an echo here of that word of doom with which Zephaniah's message began in chapter 1—"I will sweep away (literally "remove"; *asaph*) . . ." But what God promises now to remove *(asaph)* is all that is harmful. Enemies both within and outside the nation are included. In God's provision of future blessings, the weak and the disabled, the outcast and the dispossessed, are not forgotten. All are included, for God overturns the world's values as in the Magnificat. Then, as now, this particular promise, "I will bring you home" (v. 20), was one to touch the very heart of human emotions. In the plight of the weary refugees who nowadays cross our TV screens as they struggle to return to their homes, we begin to realize what it meant in ancient Israel to have such a promise. For a people who shortly after Zephaniah's time were to face deportation to Babylon, this promise was indeed precious.

A New Testament Song of God's Victory

Behold, the home of God is among mortals.
He will dwell with them as their God;
they will be his people,
and God himself will be with them;
he will wipe every tear from their eyes.
Death will be no more;
mourning and crying and pain will be no more,
for the first things have passed away.

REVELATION 21:3–4

PRAYER

Lord, grant us to share in the eternal song of praise:
"To the one seated on the throne and to the Lamb be blessing and
honor and glory and might forever and ever!"

REVELATION 5:13

A COMMUNITY IN NEED OF CHANGE

THERE IS SOMETHING refreshingly straightforward in the little book of Haggai after the complexity of Nahum, Habakkuk, and Zephaniah. Haggai's messages are brief and precisely dated, even to the day of the month. They belong to a single year, 520 B.C., and are addressed to two named leaders of the community, Zerubbabel, the governor, and Joshua, the high priest. Haggai's words have relevance both to the civic and to the religious life of the community.

Home Again from Exile

VERSE 1 SETS the scene. Immediately we notice a difference from earlier prophets. Haggai belongs to the time when the Jews had returned to their homeland after the years spent in exile in Babylon. Times had changed. The Persians overthrew Babylon with surprising speed in 539 B.C. Shortly afterward, by edict of Cyrus, the Persian king, the Jews and the deportees of other nations were allowed to return home. That was in 538 B.C., and by 520 they had had time to settle down—time enough, too, for serious problems to develop within the community. The situation of apathy that Haggai confronts—self first, God second—was vastly different from the high hopes pictured in Isaiah 40–55, which described the joyous return of the captives. By the time Haggai brings his urgent message to his countrymen, Darius has succeeded to the throne of Persia. The change in Judah's situation, from independent nation to province of the Persian empire, is reflected in the fact that the date given here relates to the reign of Darius, who occupied the Persian throne from 522 to 486 B.C. In contrast, the message of earlier prophets is customarily dated in relation to their own kings.

Now with Haggai we have a different situation—no longer a king but a governor, Zerubbabel, whose name suggests that he may have been born in Babylon (Babel), although he is of good Judean ancestry, even with royal blood in his veins. Despite some little confusion in detail (1 Chronicles 3:17–19 lists Shealtiel as uncle, not father, of Zerubbabel), he comes unmistakably of David's royal line, descended from Judah's penultimate king, Jehoiachin, or Jeconiah, as he is sometimes called. There is also the high priest Joshua. In the books of earlier prophets, no single priest is designated as "high priest," although priests are frequently addressed, often in highly critical terms.

The Unchanging God

BUT ONE THING hasn't changed. The message that Haggai brings is still "the word of the Lord." Circumstances have altered, the community is smaller, its needs are different, a new challenge is required, but still it comes with the same authority—from the Lord who addresses his people. Here is the continuity with the past after the trauma of exile; the Lord is still their God and, in their encounter with him, there is still the same demand for transformation, for a new perspective on life in which God comes first.

PRAYER

Lord, we thank you for reminding us that, change as circumstances undoubtedly will, and dark though our days may become, your voice still speaks to us. Give us listening ears, we pray.

Economic Disaster

THE COMMUNITY IS sad and apathetic; its independence has gone, the glory of its great days of empire under King David are long since past. So it is not for nothing that the prophet emphasizes the power of God; he calls him not simply "the Lord" but "the Lord of hosts" *(Yahweh sebaoth).* Whether this referred originally to the armies of Israel or to the heavenly hosts is not clear. Either way, he is a God of power and might.

The Good or the Best?

FIRST WE HEAR the people's own pessimistic words. They are making excuses, delaying to set to in earnest on rebuilding God's house, the magnificent temple Solomon had built three and a half centuries earlier, destroyed when Jerusalem fell to the Babylonian armies in 587 B.C. For the returned exiles the primary need seemed to be food and shelter, and who would quarrel with that? But has a hint of needless luxury crept in? They had built not basic homes but "well-built houses" (GNB), "paneled houses" (RSV), certainly well-roofed, substantial dwellings, while Yahweh's house lay in ruins. Their priorities were wrong. The good had become the enemy of the best. They had put God second. And the result was dissatisfaction despite all their endeavors, for something was missing at the community's heart.

Haggai and the Earlier Prophets

SEVERAL PROPHETS BEFORE the Exile, Amos and Isaiah among them, had warned the people that all the paraphernalia of sacrifice, the elaborate rituals of worship, were but an empty show if real commitment to God, in heart and life, was lacking. On the surface Haggai looks as if he is giving a diametrically opposite message—the temple-building matters supremely, it must come first. Yet at heart his message is in line with that earlier one. Haggai is no more concerned with the merely external than were the earlier prophets. But he knows well that commitment to God needs visible expression. The hopes and aspirations of the returned exiles must not be bounded by the physical and material. Their vision must be wider than comfort and prosperity for themselves.

God's word through Haggai is somber: "You that earn wages earn wages to put them into a bag with holes," a forceful comment on our own materialistic and secular age. We must give visible expression to our commitment, to the fact that the Lord is at the center of our life, for a healthy community needs to affirm that God is in its midst. Haggai knew well that the Lord was not confined to the temple. He could be worshiped everywhere, as Israel had learned while they were away in exile in Babylon. But Haggai's challenge to his contemporaries, and to us, is clear. God and his worship must come first. No department of life is excluded from that commitment.

PRAYER

Lord, help me to give you first place in my life, in my time, my energies, and my possessions, for all things are yours, and of your own do we give you.

THE REMEDY

THE REMEDY HAS two aspects: first, a look back over the years, a personal stock-taking—scrutinize your ways, evaluate them, God says. But regret for the past isn't enough. The second requirement is determination for the future, decisive action. Good resolutions are not enough—there is work to do; they need to "get their hands dirty." And so the command to Haggai's contemporaries is simple: "Go up into the hill-country, fetch timber, and build a house acceptable to me, where I can reveal my glory" (v. 8, REB). Here is God's promise to a despondent people. The key word here is "glory"—the radiance of God, his life-giving presence, in their midst, whether outwardly visible as in Solomon's temple at its dedication (1 Kings 8:11), or as in Jesus' incarnate life, ". . . we have beheld his glory" (John 1:14, RSV).

This little book of Haggai shows us, among other things, the patience of God, reasoning with his people, explaining what is wrong. Haggai, like prophets before and after him, is not afraid to speak of God in everyday terms. The people expected a great harvest, but it came to little. It was so lightweight that a puff of God's breath blew it away. The Bible portrays God's breath both as creative and life-giving, and as destructive. It was God's breath that made Adam into a living being from a blob of mud (Genesis 2:7) and resurrected the dry bones of Ezekiel's vision (Ezekiel 37:7–11), but it was also the Lord's breath (spirit/wind; *ruach YHWH*) that Hosea saw as a devastating force, a demonstration of God's power (Hosea 13:15).

In Haggai's time there was economic disaster. This, says the prophet, is God's warning to his people. Haggai doesn't recognize second causes. God, the Creator, is the sole cause of all things. It is in his power to grant or to withhold heaven's rain and earth's produce. The failure of harvest is God's doing. Yet to Haggai this is a reason for confidence, not despair. God is in control, working in human affairs, and he wants to bless his people. Haggai's stern words are in fact words of hope.

Is Haggai's message an oversimplistic one: Rebuild the temple and all will be well? Is God's blessing a mechanical response to such an external activity? Haggai's message is more honorable than that, and his view of God more spiritually empowering. The restoration of the temple would be an outward and visible sign of their determination to put God first, to make sure that worship lay at the community's heart, that the temple expressed their identity as the Yahweh community, their commitment to serve him, and him alone.

For us, too, church buildings in our villages and cities are a continual reminder that "man shall not live by bread alone" (Matthew 4:4), but the glory manifested there must spill out into the whole of life if God is to be truly honored. As Isaiah 66:1–2 reminds us, no temple is adequate for God's glory:

Heaven is my throne
and the earth is my footstool:
what is the house that you would build for me?
. . . this is the one to whom I will look,
to the humble and contrite in spirit,
who trembles at my word.

PRAYER
Lord, cleanse my heart and make it your dwelling place,
radiant with your glory.

JOYFUL ENTHUSIASM

AFTER THE APATHY and the calamities of the previous verses, what a joyful ending this is to chapter 1! It starts with obedience, an immediate, ungrudging response to God's word, and it ends with action: "They came and worked." Here is a lesson in cooperation: the two leaders Zerubbabel and Joshua working together, and not only the leaders but the people, too, in harmony. And it wasn't only human cooperation. All of them together were cooperating with God, the fount of enthusiasm with whom the initiative lay. For it was God who stirred up the spirit of Zerubbabel, of Joshua, and of the "remnant" of the people, that is, those who had returned from exile. "Remnant" is an interesting word, and to translate it simply as "the rest of the people" (as in REB) is inadequate. Nowadays it is the term often used for bargains of merchandise, usually short lengths of cloth left over. But in the Old Testament it serves to affirm that however much God's people may forget him and live their lives without him, and however much their enemies may triumph over them and deport them to a foreign country, God does not leave himself without a witness, or without the seed that will germinate into hope for the future. There is always a "remnant" of his people.

Everyone a Participant

WE SEE IN these verses the importance of our participation in God's work. He needs not only the famous and outstanding but all the unknown ordinary people. There's a place for everyone in God's service, a special task for each. But there is another name, too, listed here, without whom this chapter would not have come to such a joyful conclusion, and that is the prophet Haggai. When the people "obeyed the voice of the Lord their God," that voice had come to them through "the words of Haggai the prophet, as the Lord their God had *sent* him." Here we have Haggai's credentials, *sent (shalach)* by the Lord, the Hebrew equivalent of the Greek word from which "apostle" comes in the New Testament. Haggai knew where his authority came from, not from some superior intellectual gift of his own, but from the fact that he was the Lord's "messenger" and he spoke "with the Lord's message." And this was the power behind his words that evoked an immediate response. It was the Lord's message, not Haggai's. And that is still today the only source of the power of the Word to change human lives, to make the apathetic and indifferent, and the bewildered, too, hear and respond.

It is interesting to notice that out of these four verses and the many details they give, the message itself is brief in the extreme, just four words in English, only two in Hebrew, and yet how powerful and profound: *"I am with you,"* says the Lord (v. 13). In fact, the expression translated "says the Lord" is a particularly solemn one. Its tone is perhaps better captured by the more formal phrase, "utterance (or oracle) of the Lord."

A Life-changing Promise

HERE IS A promise to be relied on like all God's promises, a promise firm enough to stake one's all on. And with this simple yet life-changing promise the Lord stirred up leaders and people alike to accomplish his task. It was a momentous occasion, and its date is recorded. The work begun that day lasted through many centuries until destroyed by Pompey's armies in 63 B.C.

PRAYER

Lord, you have called us to dedicate ourselves to the service of your kingdom. Make us resolute and courageous in your service, strengthened by your spirit.

GOD KEEPS HIS PROMISE

THE LEADERS AND people have obeyed. Work has started on the restoration of the temple. Seven weeks after Haggai's first message he speaks again in the Lord's name. To judge from the date given here, the twenty-first day of the seventh month, this message was given to the people during the autumn harvest festival, the Feast of Tabernacles, or Booths, which we can read about in Leviticus 23:39–43. This setting is important. It is the clue to why Haggai refers to the exodus from Egypt in verse 5.

Once again the origin of the message is emphasized: It is "the word of the Lord." The name of the messenger is given, and it is Haggai. The identity of the prophet is important. Prophets were not just robots, devoid of personality, but people selected by God for a particular task in particular circumstances. He knew their personalities, their talents, and their experiences, and chose the one most suited to the task.

He Knows Our Weakness

WORK ON THE temple had started, but it was small-scale; the rebuilt temple was not going to match the magnificence of Solomon's temple. That glory had long since gone, fallen to the Babylonians. Nonetheless, the temple was still a symbol of the people's commitment to God and of his presence among them. And symbols matter, because they express spiritual truths that are independent of them yet signified by them. Our God is understanding of human weakness, as the psalmist recognized: "He knows how we were made; he remembers that we are dust" (Psalm 103:14). And so, through his prophet, God comes with a threefold word of encouragement: "Take courage . . . take courage . . . take courage." The present temple may seem as nothing in comparison with its past splendor. Yet "I am with you." And that intensely personal relationship with God, "I . . . you," is what stiffens our resolve, too, as we struggle against what sometimes seem like overwhelming odds. The oldest folk in Haggai's time may have remembered the glory of the temple half a century and more earlier, before Jerusalem fell to the Babylonians. But God's memory is longer still. Way back before the temple existed, Israel came out of Egypt. The might of the pharaoh and his armies was ranged against a slave population, but they were led by Moses—and by *God*. His promise to be with them then, not in a splendid temple but in the barren wilderness, still holds. God's promises do not fade, though temples may fall and men may die.

The Same Yesterday, Today, and Forever

THE EXODUS FROM Egypt was an ancient story of deliverance, but God is the God of today as well as of yesterday, and his promises hold firm. Appearances may be against us but one thing is sure: "My spirit abides among you" (v. 5), and it's on this basis that God says, "Do not fear." Don't look at appearances; they can be deceptive. Don't judge as the world judges. God has other values:

As the heavens are higher than the earth,
so are my ways higher than your ways
and my thoughts than your thoughts.
ISAIAH 55:9

It is his presence with us that makes all the difference.

PRAYER

Lord, grant that I may begin to see with your eyes, to judge as you judge, and to live in the new dimension that your presence gives.

LOOK TO THE FUTURE

THREE TIMES IN our last passage Haggai repeated, "Take courage!" Everyone was to be involved, the leaders and the people too. And here now is the reason for that confidence. God is in control, and all the wealth of all the earth, the riches of all the nations, are his. The rebuilt temple of this impoverished community could not stand comparison with Solomon's magnificent edifice built at a time of Israel's political greatness. Nonetheless, it symbolized God's presence and power among them, just as he had been with them in the wilderness when they were a homeless people and their place of worship was a movable tent, the tabernacle.

The prophet speaks in glowing terms of the future splendor of God's house. It is not altogether clear why the word "shake" is used (v. 6). It may be a picture drawn from everyday life when storms of ferocious wind could so easily shake the ripened fruit from the trees. However, some commentators have associated it with historical events of the time, in particular the upheavals that took place in the Persian Empire in the years 522–521, as rivals struggled for the throne. But whatever lies behind the image, it is clear that the enrichment of the temple will take place only by Yahweh's initiative. As always, the Old Testament is mindful that Yahweh's coming is not a comfortable, cozy experience. It means upheaval and disturbance whether he comes with judgment or salvation.

A second point to notice is the inclusion of all nations. All are under his sovereign sway, and one nation alone cannot sufficiently offer the gifts of which he is worthy.

As often in prophetic visions, there is a foreshortening of the timescale; "once again, in a little while . . . ," just as there is in the earliest writings of the New Testament (for example, 1 Thessalonians 5) in the expectation of Christ's imminent return.

The Promise Reinterpreted

HAGGAI'S MESSAGE LED his contemporaries to look forward to what God had in store for them in the future, not back with nostalgia to what seemed like greater days gone forever. As time went by, their hopes had to be reinterpreted and the picture language received no literal fulfillment.

And so it is for us. The promise points Christians on to a fulfillment of Haggai's words different from any that he might have envisaged. In the gospel story, Christians are reminded of that humble dwelling to which the Gentiles' gifts were brought, when a stable became the dwelling place of God incarnate. Early Christian commentators, mindful of this echo in the gospel, interpreted "the treasure of all nations" (v. 7) as the promised Messiah himself.

The final promise of this passage is God's gift of *shalom.* How are we adequately to translate into English this rich Hebrew word? "Prosperity," says NRSV; "prosperity and peace," says REB, for certainly more than material prosperity is intended. It is well-being in its deepest sense, the renewal of relationships between people and, above all, between people and God.

PRAYER

Lord, we thank you that, although all the wealth of earth and heaven is yours, you laid it aside to share the life of the humble and poor, the homeless and the outcast, and that in you they, too, can be enriched.

IS HOLINESS CONTAGIOUS?

HAGGAI'S MESSAGE CHANGES abruptly. From the visionary and the prophetic it becomes practical, of direct relevance to everyday life. To us this seems a strange discussion on an abstruse point of law. It is in fact a direct challenge to the people about the reality of their individual relationship to God.

The strange questions are posed to the priests, for it was one of their main tasks to interpret God's law and to instruct the people in it. The discussion centers on the contrasting ideas of holiness and uncleanness. Is what is true of one also true of the other, as regards their transmission? The priests can give the authoritative answer.

By this time the people had been working for three months to rebuild the temple. They were growing discouraged again, and once more Haggai has to challenge them, this time from a different perspective. Is holiness contagious? That is the first question. The answer is clear: Holiness cannot be transmitted from one thing or from one person to another. The temple has been rebuilt and the regular sacrificial rituals reinstated. These things are holy, but can that holiness be transmitted to the worshipers? The answer is no. These holy things cannot of themselves confer holiness. Personal commitment and obedience to God are fundamental requirements of the spiritual life, to be expressed in outward rituals but never replaced by them.

An unjustified criticism is sometimes leveled against Haggai: that, unlike the earlier prophets, his primary concern is with rituals and ceremonies. He is aware that the external symbols and institutions of worship are important as the focal point of the community, binding its members together and giving them identity, but without the personal commitment of their lives to God, these things are worthless. To suppose that God responds to merely outward observances, without the transformation of the worshipers, is a denial of his very nature as the Lord who calls his people into a covenant relationship with him.

Is Uncleanness Contagious?

HAGGAI'S SECOND QUESTION, "Is uncleanness contagious?" receives an emphatic affirmative. This is true, of course, not only in matters of ritual uncleanness but in medical and hygienic terms. Health cannot be passed from one to another; it is not transmissible, but diseases of many kinds are all too readily transmitted. The same is true of moral contagion. It is catching. It spreads quietly and unobserved. Even the holy offerings, says Haggai, are rendered unclean by the uncleanness of the worshipers, a startling condemnation of those who had rebuilt the temple and reinstituted the regular offerings after the disruption of the deportation and exile.

Yet despite their continued unfaithfulness to the Lord, there is always with God the possibility of a new beginning: "From this day on I will bless you."

PRAYER
Lord, help us to learn the lessons of your holy word
and to make a fresh start today, renewing our commitment to you
and seeking your blessing.

THE MESSIAH FORESHADOWED

THE BOOK OF Haggai ends on a visionary note, a reminder that the words of the prophets, those mysterious messengers from God, were relevant not only to their immediate contemporaries. Born out of particular historical circumstances, they were not limited to those but embraced the future, hinting in impressionistic form at what was yet to be. Logic, with its cold parameters of human reason, is at odds with the prophets who spoke of a greater, yet unseen, reality. Haggai had earlier told of the wealth of nations flowing into the temple to beautify it, a reminder that all earth's wealth, and heaven's too, belongs to the Lord. But here kingdoms, nations, and all the trappings of their power and rule are to be overthrown. Those who have lived by the sword will ultimately die by the sword. Haggai was not a political agitator. He was not speaking in literal, historical terms of disturbances within the Persian Empire, but of God's action on a grander scale against all that opposes his rule. This is a scene not of human making. Haggai turns again to his earlier expression, "I am about to shake the heavens and the earth" (v. 21). This is entirely God's doing, without human intervention. Amid the wreckage of earth's empires, God's kingdom stands, eternal and without comparison.

The Suffering Servant

GREAT HOPES FOR the future were centered on Zerubbabel, for he was a descendant of David's royal house. The terms applied to him here are messianic; he is God's chosen servant, the one with his kingly authority, as it were his "signet ring." The king's signet, by which letters and edicts were sealed, conferred upon them the king's authority, just as truly as if the king himself were present in person. But Zerubbabel soon disappeared from the stage of history. We have no knowledge of what later befell him. For its ultimate fulfillment the promise had to await the coming of another Son of David's royal line, no other than Jesus. But this chosen Messiah was destined also to fulfill another prophet's vision, of the suffering servant "wounded for our transgressions, crushed for our iniquities; by his bruises we are healed" (Isaiah 53:5).

Haggai had spoken of the treasure of all nations filling God's house with splendor (2:7). In symbolic fashion, the gospel story tells of wise men coming from eastern lands to bring their treasures—gold, frankincense, and myrrh—to the one in whom God's presence most truly dwelt.

Haggai's words of encouragement and hope come to an abrupt end. His vision was restricted, time-bound, relating to a particular circumstance. His hopes were fulfilled not in material but in spiritual terms. But the gospel of the Messiah whom Zerubbabel foreshadowed is universal in its scope and eternal in its relevance:

His dominion is an everlasting dominion,
that shall not pass away,
and his kingship is one that shall never be destroyed.
DANIEL 7:14

PRAYER
Lord, we thank you for the fulfillment of the visions and hopes of many centuries when Christ came, your royal Son born in a stable, suffering on a cross, and now enthroned in glory, and all this because he loves us with an everlasting love.

A VISIONARY PROPHET

THE IMMEDIATE IMPRESSION we gain on opening the book of Zechariah is that here is a sequel to Haggai. In fact, the dates overlap. Zechariah's ministry belongs to the years 520–518 B.C., when Judah was a province of the Persian Empire, hence the date is given with reference to the reign of Darius, the Persian king. The superficial similarity to the book of Haggai is, however, deceptive. After the first few verses we are plunged into a series of eight strange visions, each one more mysterious than the last. Zechariah, it seems, is not only the longest book of the twelve "minor" prophets, it is also the strangest! But if we seek we shall find! The language is symbolic, the visions are bizarre, but as part of holy scripture they are not to be lightly dismissed. Read with a sensitive imagination, they challenge and disturb as well as encourage us. The prophet's message took root in his particular historical circumstances, but always it reaches beyond the immediate and the mundane to speak of eternal things.

God's Coming Kingdom

AFTER THE FIRST eight chapters we leave behind the visions and the historical setting in Darius' reign and move on two centuries or more to the late fourth or early third century B.C. There are no dates given in chapters 9–14 and Zechariah himself disappears from view. The language of these chapters, too, is highly symbolic; but despite their obscurity they are of particular interest for Christians, since they are quoted several times at significant points in the gospel narratives and are applied to Christ's suffering and death.

Here are messages, complex and bizarre though they may seem, that give us food for thought and a challenge to faith—to trust God amid the complexities of the world and find encouragement in his unchanging will to save. There are glimpses here of God's coming kingdom and of its glory.

A Lesson from History

ZECHARIAH DOESN'T GO in for an attractive introduction, or flattering words, to get his audience's attention. He plunges straight in: "Return to me, says the Lord of hosts, and I will return to you." Look back at history, he urges them, and learn its lessons. Past generations ignored the warnings of prophets such as Isaiah and Micah, and later Jeremiah, and exile had been the result. And so Zechariah underlines the authority of his urgent message. Three times he repeats, ". . . says the Lord of hosts." It seems a strange beginning to a message intended to encourage a downcast people trying to reestablish themselves in their homeland after years of exile. But the call to repentance is the framework for God's promise of a new and better future. Remember how Jesus began his ministry of *good news:* "The kingdom of God has come near; *repent,* and believe" (Mark 1:15).

Learn a lesson from history, says Zechariah. People and prophets are transient, but God's word lives on.

To Think Over

All flesh is like grass and all its glory like the flower of grass. The grass withers and the flower falls, but the word of the Lord endures forever.

1 PETER 1:25

REPENTANCE AND RENEWAL

THE DATE GIVEN here is still more precise than that in verse 1. Its effect is to emphasize the significance of the occasion. For the prophet it was a memorable experience. Zechariah was not the first prophet to receive God's message through a vision—it happened to Isaiah and Jeremiah, and to Amos too, among others. But Zechariah's visions were different. They came to him in the quiet of the night and most of them were not the stuff of which ordinary life is made. So strange were the visions that Zechariah needed an interpreting angel to help him make sense of them.

The expression "in the night" (v. 8) is significant. It reminds us that prophets are sometimes compared to watchmen (Ezekiel 3:17), whose task it was to watch over the city through the long hours of darkness (Psalm 130:6). In the quietness of the night, when the day's bustling activity was over, God spoke to Zechariah. But these were not dreams coming unbidden to the prophet while he slept. They were waking visions demanding his full attention. On one occasion he had to be wakened by the angel (4:1). Just as Habakkuk had to wait patiently for God's answer, so for Zechariah, too, there was an element of patient waiting, not only in the night but through years of exile and the disillusionment that followed, until at last here was God's answer, a promise of compassion and restoration.

A Divine Intercessor

NOT ALL THE participants in the conversation are clearly identified. There is a mysterious "man" riding on a red horse, and a "man" standing among the myrtle trees. An angel, too, stands among the trees. It all has a somewhat dreamlike quality and, like the parables Jesus told, not every detail carries equal significance. But the climax of the vision comes when the angel makes intercession for the people and the Lord replies "with gracious and comforting words." Here in Zechariah is an angelic intercessor pleading on behalf of a troubled and distressed community. And we, too, when we are aware of the weakness of our own praying, know that we have a divine intercessor, the Holy Spirit himself, pleading for us "with sighs too deep for words" (Romans 8:26).

Despite the mysterious quality of the vision, its main elements derive from actual life. Mounted patrols reminiscent of the Persian Empire figure in it, as do myrtle trees, evoked, no doubt, by the trees growing in the temple forecourt. Myrtles were among the highly prized trees in ancient Israel and are listed with cedar, acacia, and olive in the lovely portrayal of desert transformed into fertile land (Isaiah 41:19). Zechariah's vision pictures the nations at peace, suggesting that the political upheavals that occurred at the beginning of Darius' reign are over. The seventy years represent a whole lifetime of distress through the years of exile (586–538 B.C.) and the earlier deportations.

God at Work in the World

THE OLD TESTAMENT envisages God at work in and through the affairs of nations, but it also recognizes human free will. This is what lies behind the rather quaint expression "while I was only a little angry, they [the nations] made the disaster worse" (v. 15). Disasters are not naively attributed to God by the prophet. God works through the events of history but the nations are nonetheless accountable for their actions.

Zechariah's God is not distant or aloof but passionately concerned for his people. This theological affirmation is expressed by the word "jealous," a biblical term often misunderstood as a petty, unworthy emotion. The Good News Bible captures the meaning: "I have a deep love and concern for Jerusalem, my holy city" (v. 14). The "measuring line" of verse 16, a builder's tool, implies that the restoration of Jerusalem will be brought to completion. We shall meet this idea again in the third vision.

TO THINK OVER
Judgment is not God's final word. His purpose is salvation,
but salvation is no cheap and easy option. It involves a change
of direction, a radical transformation.

DESTRUCTION DESTROYED

THE SECOND VISION, more compact and less complex though it is than the first, resembles it in its question-and-answer form. But this time there are only two participants in the dialogue, the prophet and the angelic interpreter, the Lord's spokesman. It is, if anything, more bizarre than the first vision: Four apparently unattached powerful horns (probably oxen horns are intended) represent the world's brutal, destructive power. Then the Lord (Zechariah is profoundly conscious of the source of his vision) shows him four men, workmen equipped to work in metal or wood ("blacksmiths" is a good equivalent), whose task is to destroy the horns and thus to overcome the destructive power of the nations the horns represent.

God Omnipresent

THE NATIONS ARE not named, but a glimpse at Israel's history might suggest that Assyria and Babylon, Egypt and Persia, could be in mind. Each of them had played a part over the centuries in defeating Israel, and from the eighth century onward Israel's life had been dominated by powerful nations. First the northern kingdom had fallen to Assyria toward the end of the eighth century, then a century and a half later Judah was conquered by Babylon and the leaders among its population deported to what is now Iraq. Egypt, too, had been a powerful enemy, and in Zechariah's time the Persian Empire was dominant.

Some, on the other hand, have attempted to identify the horns with four Babylonian rulers. More likely, however, the four horns represent the four points of the compass. From whatever direction danger might threaten God's people, he is omnipresent and omnipotent, sovereign over all the world.

Faith's Affirmation

BUT WHY DOES the prophet not identify more clearly the other figures in the vision, the blacksmiths who are to bring deliverance to God's people?

The details, as in all the visions, are imprecise, and deliberately so. For the message entrusted to Zechariah is not about past history but a courageous affirmation that God is Lord of the present and the future. This is a vision born of faith that God is mightier than every human power, come what may.

This passage expresses, no less confidently than the first vision, that God is not remote from his people's distress but is passionately concerned for them. Yet to take it as undiluted nationalism is seriously to misinterpret it. The opening verses of Zechariah have made clear in their call for repentance that God's people, too, stand under judgment and are accountable to him for their actions. But the prophet is convinced that God's time for deliverance will come. His confidence rests not on human reason but on divine revelation. The Hebrew reads literally, *"the Lord caused me to see* four workmen."

For us, too, it is only the vision of faith, not a reasoned and practical assessment of life's hazards, that makes it possible for us to affirm, in face of every appearance to the contrary, that "the kingdom of the world *has become* the kingdom of our Lord and of his Messiah, and he will reign forever and ever" (Revelation 11:15).

God's Promise

You who live in the shelter of the Most High,
who abide in the shadow of the Almighty,
will say to the Lord, "My refuge and my fortress;
my God, in whom I trust."

PSALM 91:1–2

PRAYER

Lord, grant us the gift of faith to trust your love even in our darkest moments, and to know your presence with us, whatever befalls.

JERUSALEM, CITY WITHOUT WALLS

THIS IS A splendid vision, one of the high points of the book of Zechariah. It looks beyond the restoration of the earthly Jerusalem to God's coming kingdom and a holy city with no walls to keep out the uninvited, no exclusion of "foreigners," for all are welcomed as citizens. The builder's measuring line, mentioned obscurely in the first vision, reappears. Jerusalem's capacity to make room for the inhabitants of God's open city is to be measured. For the returned exiles of Zechariah's time this is an assurance that Jerusalem, still bearing the marks of enemy attack, will be restored. Its inhabitants, diminished in number by the aftereffects of deportation and exile, will be replenished. But this is a prophetic word with broader vision too. The rebuilding of Jerusalem is symbolic of God's future reign and his all-embracing city.

God's Welcome for All

THIS TIME THERE are more participants in the conversation. Beside the prophet there is a "man" holding the measuring line; there are also two angels. Again there is the dreamlike quality we have come to expect in the visions. The man with the measuring line has no doubts about his task. It is clearly defined, factual, and technical; he is about to measure the extent of Jerusalem. Then comes a sudden interruption, a change of plan. Things are not quite what they seem, and there is urgency about the next move. For the interpreting angel himself becomes a participant in the action. Another angel gives him instructions, an urgent message to stop the architect in his tracks. For his plans are too small, too closely restricted by the bounds of human logic, for God's city is immeasurable. The angel is to run and warn him that God's new Jerusalem has no need of walls either to keep its inhabitants in or to keep their enemies out. So immense will be the number of persons and animals at home within it that the city will burst at the seams. Walls are impossible! And yet the city will have its defenses, for God's kingdom will still have its enemies—all those who oppose his just and gentle rule. No human resource will be sufficient. God makes a promise to his own, and a thrilling one it is: "I will be a wall of fire all around it, says the Lord, and I will be the glory within it." A *wall* of fire—remember the *pillar* of fire that guided God's people through the wilderness by night to the promised land.

Continuity and Change

THERE IS CONTINUITY with the past. God is still the same God, yesterday, today, and forever, but there is newness, too, in God's plans for the future. We need to build on the past, to restore what has been destroyed, to recapture what has been lost; but stopping there denies God's purpose. He calls us to reach out adventurously, neither hampered by past failures nor lulled into complacency by past successes, to think that what has been must ever be. God is a God of change, of growth, of untold blessing. There is room in his kingdom for everyone who responds to his invitation.

Not many years after Zechariah's vision, Nehemiah set about rebuilding Jerusalem's walls, excluding outsiders in order to maintain the identity of the little postexilic community. Vision is sometimes lost in the exigencies of history and Nehemiah's actions, courageous as they were, were necessary to meet the problems of the time. But the vision, though lost for a time, was not obliterated, and it reappears in the New Testament when all are bidden to the feast in Jesus' parable (Luke 14:15–24). The only ones excluded were those whose excuses rejected the invitation.

PRAYER

Lord, grant that the limits of our vision may not restrict your actions and your will to save.

THE APPLE OF HIS EYE

SUDDENLY THE TONE changes. No recounting of a visionary experience this time but an urgent summons to the people who remain in exile, an appropriate sequel to the vision of the unwalled Jerusalem, a city without walls, with room for multitudes. In place of the interpreting angel, God's human messenger, the prophet, speaks, calling the remaining exiles to come home from "the land of the north," Babylon. Although, strictly speaking, Babylon lay to the east of Israel, the terrain was such that the route from Babylon entered Judah from the north and it is often referred to in these terms.

The summons is accompanied by the statement that it was the Lord himself who "spread you abroad like the four winds of heaven" (v. 6). In this lies the authority of the summons, for the God who scattered his people is able also to gather them and bring them home. This is no arbitrary God but one who acts according to his word established in the covenant made at Sinai. It is not the power of hostile nations but the power of God that has shaped Israel's history, says the prophet. And it is in his hands that their future lies.

A Fresh Start

NOW IS THE time for a new beginning, for joy and singing. That's what God longs to hear from his redeemed people, and the reason for their joy is that God's own presence is with them. "Sing and rejoice, O daughter Zion! For lo, I will come and dwell in your midst, says the Lord" (v. 10), surely an echo of Psalm 46. And what a courageous psalm that is: "God is our refuge and strength, a very present help in trouble. *Therefore* we will not fear" (Psalm 46:1–2) . . . all because "God is in the midst of the city."

Here is God's involvement with his people, no distant, self-sufficient God but vulnerable to his people's suffering: "Truly, one who touches you touches the apple of my eye" (v. 8) (literally the "baby," the small image reflected in the eye). And there is room, too, in God's city for people of other nations. They, too, will be his people. There is no place here for racial discrimination in the thought of Zechariah. Interestingly, we have in this passage the only Old Testament occurrence of that now-familiar phrase, "the holy land."

Our passage ends on a different note from the joy and singing that have gone before, but this is no less an expression of worship: "Be silent before the Lord," a phrase doubtless drawn from Israel's liturgy. This God, who is so close to his people that they are the very "apple of his eye," is the great, transcendent, holy God. There is a time for singing and a time for silence before the mystery of his awesome presence. To overstress one of these aspects of worship at the expense of the other diminishes our offering and devalues God.

PRAYER

Lord, in the midst of our busy lives, grant us to find that hallowed space where, in silence before you, we may worship in awe and wonder at your glory and your grace.

GUILT REMOVED

Readers using the NEB should note that the visions have been rearranged: 4:1–3, 11–14 have been inserted between chapters 2 and 3 to create what the translators regarded as a more logical order.

THE FOCUS OF this curious vision is Joshua the high priest, who was contemporary with Zechariah. The scene presented is set in the heavenly realm, although its features reflect the historical circumstances of the time. After the exile the office of high priest took on a greater prominence. In place of the monarchy, which ended with the Exile, the high priest became the civil as well as the religious leader of the community.

This fourth vision differs in its pattern from the previous ones. There is no interpreting angel here and no conversation with the prophet. The latter's only interjection according to the Hebrew text, "Let them put a clean turban on his head," is attributed in several English translations to the angel. The drama takes place between two conflicting angels, one of them called the Satan, that is the Adversary, the accuser of humankind (not the devil in the developed sense of evil personified that it has in the New Testament). But the central figure is a human one, the high priest Joshua, a familiar figure to Zechariah's first readers.

God's Heavenly Council

THE IDEA OF a heavenly council occurs in several places in the Old Testament. The best-known example comes in the first two chapters of the book of Job. There, the Satan is among the divine beings who present themselves before the Lord to give account of their doings. The Satan casts doubt on Job's integrity and from this ensues the story of Job's suffering and his final vindication by God. Here in Zechariah the prophet is admitted in his vision to the heavenly council. A controversy has arisen. The Adversary stands ready with his accusations. What hope would there be for Joshua if the Lord had not intervened with the offer of a way of cleansing and the opportunity for renewal? The rebuke administered to Satan reminds us of Jesus' stern response, "Get behind me, Satan!" when Peter would have turned him back from the way of the cross and of our redemption (Mark 8:33).

Joshua is reclothed in fresh garments, a symbol that his guilt is purged and he is fit to stand before God as mediator for the people. The prophet shares in the act of renewal, urging that a clean turban be placed on Joshua's head. The high priest's headdress is associated specifically with atonement in the description of the priestly garments (Exodus 28:38). Like a piece of wood snatched from the fire, priest and people have been delivered from the trauma of exile. God has a future for them, cleansed and forgiven, ready for his service.

MEDITATION

Read meditatively Hebrews 4:15–16 and rejoice in Jesus (the Greek form of the Hebrew name Joshua), our High Priest, sinless himself, yet the friend of sinners.

We have not a high priest who is unable to sympathize with our weaknesses, but one who in every respect has been tempted as we are, yet without sin. Let us then with confidence draw near to the throne of grace, that we may receive mercy and find grace to help in time of need (RSV).

THE GOSPEL IN A NUTSHELL

DESPITE THE STRANGE language and content of this vision, we have here what might be called the gospel in a nutshell. From filthy garments, Joshua is given a "spotless robe of righteousness," not because of any merit on his part, but because of God's mercy, even in the face of Satan's accusations. Here is forgiveness, cleansing offered by God. But it is not a cheap and easy way of grace. There is a moral imperative. Joshua is under an obligation thereafter to obey, to live out in his life what God has so freely offered him: "If you will walk in my ways and keep my requirements, then . . ."

God Makes a Promise

JOSHUA WILL HAVE the right of access, communion with God, and so will those whom he represents as priest. We can compare this with the New Testament picture of Jesus as our "high priest," through whom alone we have the right of access into God's holy presence, for there is "one mediator between God and humankind, Christ Jesus, himself human, who gave himself a ransom for all" (1 Timothy 2:5).

The significance of the stone set before Joshua is obscure, but its seven facets indicate completeness and perfection. The number seven is used frequently with this significance in the Old Testament. Possibly the stone is envisaged as attached to the mitre, or turban, worn by Joshua as high priest, which according to the instructions given in Exodus 28:36 bore the inscription "Holy to the Lord." All this, says our passage, is a sign of yet more to come, the promise of a great and glorious future, the coming of God's Messiah, here called the Branch (v. 8). And what lovelier picture could there be than the rural idyll with which this vision ends, a picture of peace and plenty, each one under his "vine and fig tree," a familiar Old Testament symbol of blessing. And this is not selfish indulgence enjoyed in isolation; it is gladness and prosperity shared with one another in community. Is this itself perhaps a salutary reminder to us?

Another Promise

THERE IS THE promise, too, of guilt removed "in a single day" (v. 9). Underlying this is an allusion to the great Day of Atonement celebrated once every year, when the high priest symbolically made an offering on behalf of all the people to atone for their sin. You will find the details in Leviticus 16, especially verses 20–22. But as we have seen already, the prophet's vision extends beyond the immediate into the future and carries a yet more profound meaning. In a remarkable way these strange words of Zechariah foreshadow the coming of Christ, both priest and king, and, amazing wonder, himself the atoning sacrifice. The unqualified and absolute nature of Zechariah's phrase "in a single day" points us on to the epistle to the Hebrews, where the uniqueness of Christ's priesthood is set out. He is not a high priest who needs to enter year by year into the sanctuary to make atonement for sin: "He has appeared *once for all* at the climax of history to abolish sin by the sacrifice of himself" (Hebrews 9:26, REB, italics added).

MEDITATION AND PRAYER

Read Hebrews 9:11–14 and give thanks for Christ's perfect sacrifice by which all our sins are forgiven and our burden of guilt taken away.

Lord God, we want to thank you for the gift of Jesus to be our Savior. Help us to live in the light of his love and forgiveness, and to share that love with other people.

EVERY MOUNTAIN AND HILL
SHALL BE MADE LOW

Readers using the REB should note that verses 1–3 have been transposed to follow verse 10.

THE PREVIOUS VISION focused on Joshua the high priest. Now attention turns to the temple. A seven-branched golden candlestick stood in the temple, but this lampstand is an altogether more elaborate structure. Try to picture it. There is a bowl on top of the stand with seven lamps, and each lamp has seven "lips," a word of uncertain meaning but probably signifying places to hold the wicks rather than pipes for the oil. Thus there are forty-nine lights glowing on this "lampstand all of gold." And at each side of it stands an olive tree. What the lamps and the olive trees symbolize is not explained in this passage. There is a hint further on in the chapter of another meaning: The lamp seems to symbolize the omnipresence of God, and we shall consider this later. In the book of Revelation, where the risen Christ in his glory appears to John in exile on the island of Patmos, the seven lampstands explicitly represent the seven churches to whom the messages are addressed. The possibility arises that the golden lampstand of Zechariah's vision represents Israel, whose vocation is to give light to the nations, an idea in tune with the famous words in Isaiah 60:1 and 3:

> *Arise, shine; for your light has come,*
> *and the glory of the Lord has risen upon you . . .*
> *Nations shall come to your light,*
> *and kings to the brightness of your dawn.*

If this is the correct interpretation, the significance of the olive trees becomes clear. They represent the two leaders, Joshua and Zerubbabel, on whom depends the future of the community and the restoration of its worship with the temple at its heart.

A Promise for all Time

THE VISION IS interrupted by a message for Zerubbabel, who figured so prominently in the book of Haggai. Despite strong opposition on the part of some in the community ("a great mountain") Zerubbabel will succeed in restoring the temple. And what a promise he is given, one that leaves no room for human pride: "Not by might, nor by power but by my spirit, says the Lord of hosts" (v. 6). Some had disparaged the rebuilding of the temple as "the day of small things" (v. 10). But whatever is done to the glory of God is precious, and when the last stone is brought out to be set into its place, the onlookers will shout, "Beautiful, beautiful!" (v. 7)

To Think Over

"WHAT ARE YOU, O great mountain? . . . you shall become a plain" (v. 7). God's promise reaches beyond Zerubbabel and that ancient time to all who seek to serve him.

The New Testament expresses it in different words but the promise is the same: "If you say to this mountain, 'Be lifted up and thrown into the sea,' it will be done. Whatever you ask for in prayer with faith, you will receive" (Matthew 21:21–22).

Yet alongside this we need to set Paul's warning, "If I have all faith, so as to remove mountains, but do not have love, I am nothing" (1 Corinthians 13:2).

PRAYER

Lord, we thank you for your promise that it is not by human power but by your Spirit that we can victoriously serve you.

PATIENCE TO WATCH
AND WAIT AND PRAY

Readers using the Good News Bible should note that verses 10b–14 have been transposed to follow verse 5.

ANOTHER MESSAGE COMES from the Lord to Zerubbabel, this time through the prophet. Only then is the meaning of the vision explained. This gives the chapter a rather disjointed appearance, hence the rearrangement of the verses in some of our translations. The REB takes the "seven eyes of the Lord" to refer to the seven facets ("eyes") of the stone set before Joshua at the end of chapter 3, hence its reordering of the verses. As the text stands, however (and this is made even clearer by the Good News Bible's rearrangement), the sevenfold lamps on the lampstand represent the seven eyes of the all-seeing God whose eyes "range through the whole earth." "Nothing in creation can hide from him; everything lies bare and exposed to the eyes of him to whom we must render account," says the writer to the Hebrews (4:13, REB).

Agents in God's Service

YET IF THE lampstand with its seven lamps represents God in his omniscience, we are left wondering, as Zechariah was, what is the function of the two olive trees that stand beside it. If, as seemed likely earlier in the chapter, the lamps represented Israel in its role as bringer of light to the other nations, then the olive trees providing fuel for the lamps were an appropriate symbol for the leaders whose encouragement provided the impetus for the community's task of reestablishing its identity and restoring the temple as the heart of its worship. But the omnipresent, all-sufficient God has no need of "olive trees" to provide oil for his "lamp." No wonder the bewildered prophet has to put his question a second time to the interpreting angel! The olive trees still represent the leaders, Joshua and Zerubbabel, "the anointed ones," but this time their function is different: They "stand by the Lord of the whole earth" as his agents to fulfill his purpose for humankind.

Is the chapter disorganized? True, it seems as if two different interpretations are given of the significance of the golden lampstand. But we must remember both that this is an ancient text and not to be judged by modern standards of what is logical, and also that as a word from God it is dynamic and may be reinterpreted and applied to new generations. Questions as to how the text took shape, important and interesting though they are, point us to the past. But the message and the challenge it brings root us in the present and encourage us for the future, disturbing us when complacent and inspiring us when tempted to despair. The text reminds us that answers to our perplexities do not always come immediately. Sometimes we have to wait for God's reply. This was true of the prophet Jeremiah (42:7). It was true, too, of Habakkuk, as we discovered earlier in our study. And for patient waiting we need God's strength.

MEDITATION AND PRAYER

Even youths shall faint and be weary,
and young men shall fall exhausted;
but they who wait for the Lord shall renew their strength,
they shall mount up with wings like eagles,
they shall run and not be weary,
they shall walk and not faint.

ISAIAH 40:30–31, RSV

Lord, grant us the patience that waits on you in good times and in bad, and joyful hearts to praise you in the certainty of faith. Give us open minds, ready and willing to understand and receive your holy word and to live by it in daily life.

A COMMUNITY TRANSFORMED

THIS SIXTH VISION, the flying scroll, reads strangely to modern ears. It is, if anything, more bizarre than the last. Once again the prophet looks up and sees an extraordinary sight. "What do you see?" asks the angel. The prophet, as before, is not permitted to be a silent, passive onlooker—an answer is expected; he is a participator. Dialogue in learning is not a new technique!

The scroll was of huge dimensions, approximately fifteen feet by thirty, hinting at the extent of the community's ills. Its flight through the air suggests both that it came from the heavenly realm and that it came quickly with no obstacles in its way. The prophet Ezekiel, earlier in the sixth century, in his commissioning as a prophet, had an equally strange vision in which he was given a scroll to consume. Zechariah's vision may have been influenced by that earlier account, for several times he refers to the "former prophets" (e.g. 1:4). Like Ezekiel's scroll, Zechariah's had writing on the front and the back; the indictment was complete.

The Covenant Broken

THE REBUILDING OF the temple marked a new beginning in the community's life, a renewed commitment to worship the Lord. But for this it needed inward cleansing too. The later prophets, like their pre-exilic forebears, were convinced that the externals of worship were void without commitment of life. The idea of a written curse descending on a people is strange to us, but when Israel entered into covenant relationship with God at Mount Sinai, they put themselves under oath, a solemn promise to observe God's law. This was their side of the relationship, willingly accepted in response to God's gracious deliverance of them from Egypt. This was not a "religion of works," the attempt to earn God's favor by meritorious actions. It was the response of gratitude for what God had already done freely for them: "I am the Lord your God, who brought you out of the land of Egypt, out of the house of slavery." These words preface the Ten

Commandments in Exodus 20:2 and Deuteronomy 5:6, showing that the motivation for obedience to God's law was this relationship of gratitude and dependence.

Two specific infringements of God's law were written on the scroll that Zechariah saw in his vision, stealing and swearing falsely in his name, breaches of the eighth and third commandments. But why single out these two sins in particular? The historical situation of the time doubtless underlies it. The return from exile had created tensions between the deportees and those who had remained in the land. It is likely that "theft" refers particularly to those who refused to surrender property to its rightful owners now returned from exile, and "swearing falsely" to the corrupt lawsuits by which the owners were frustrated from recovering what was their due.

To Think Over

THE NEW TESTAMENT regards sin in the worshiping community just as seriously as does the Old Testament. We are each accountable for our infringements of God's law. But there is a different remedy to rid us of our guilt: "God shows his love for us in that while we were yet sinners, Christ died for us" (Romans 5:8, RSV).

PRAYER

Lord, we confess to you our sins in penitence and faith. Deliver us and grant us your forgiveness, not according to our merits but according to your immeasurable love shown to us in Jesus.

EVIL BANISHED

THERE FOLLOWS ANOTHER equally extraordinary vision symbolizing the extermination of evil from the community. There is, however, a difference of emphasis here: The previous vision was concerned with judgment on individual wrongdoers; this time it concerns the elimination of corruption from the whole community. Rather than dismissing this passage as totally bizarre, let us treat it as if it were a cartoon. We are all familiar with political cartoons, for example, quite as bizarre as this, which, if they were to be taken literally, would be simply ridiculous. Yet, set within a particular context and viewed against the background of contemporary events or controversial issues, they speak more powerfully than any written column and are often of more lasting impact. Of such a kind is Zechariah's vision. There is no excuse to dismiss it as a meaningless fantasy.

This time the pattern changes a little. The angel takes the initiative and urges the prophet to look up and see what is coming. But once again the prophet is bewildered: "What is it?" he asks, as well he might. It is an "ephah," a measure for corn or liquid in the form of a basket or barrel large enough to hold about nine gallons' worth. And over the top of the basket is a leaden cover, heavy enough to secure the contents. And surprise, surprise! Inside is a woman who, the moment the lid is lifted, tries to force her way out. "This is Wickedness," explains the interpreting angel, thrusting the figure back into its basket and pressing down the leaden cover. Hardly an image to appeal to women!

The Community Purged

WHY IS WICKEDNESS represented like this? There may be some connection with the pagan goddess, the "Queen of Heaven," worshiped by the women of Judah after the fall of Jerusalem, and castigated by Jeremiah (44:25–27). In any event, the word for "wickedness" in Hebrew is feminine, but before we rush to false conclusions about negative attitudes toward women, we should note that Wisdom, too, is personified as a woman in the book of Proverbs. There are other women, too, in the vision whose presence is less easily explained. With powerful wings like a stork's (another feminine noun) they lift the heavy basket and carry it off to Shinar, an old name for Babylon, which Israel in exile had discovered to be a land of many gods and goddesses. Here, says Zechariah ironically, is another to add to the number! A temple is to be built and the basket set within on a pedestal—for worship. The wickedness envisaged here seems, to judge from the context, to be idolatry in particular, the worship of anything other than God that lends a false perspective to life, to all its values and its actions. If only society's evils, its injustice and its ruthlessness, were so easily banished from our communities as they appeared to be in Zechariah's vision!

This strange vision of the public removal of sin through a symbolic action may have its origin in the ancient Israelite ritual of the scapegoat on the Day of Atonement. After a priest had laid his hands on the head of the goat in a symbolic transference of the nation's sins, the goat was let loose into the desert to carry the guilt far away (Leviticus 16:21–22). But alongside this annual ritual of atonement on behalf of the whole community, sacrifices were offered continually for sins committed day by day.

We, too, need a break with the past, a fresh start—"new birth" Jesus called it in his conversation with Nicodemus (John 3:3)—and thereafter daily forgiveness. We are reminded of Jesus' words to Peter when he was indignant at the thought that Jesus, his Lord and Master, should wash his feet: "Unless I wash you, you have no share with me." Simon Peter said to him, "Lord, not my feet only but also my hands and my head!" Jesus said to him, "One who has bathed does not need to wash, except for the feet, but is entirely clean" (John 13:8–10).

PRAYER
Thank you, Lord, for the forgiveness and the daily cleansing that you offer us through the atoning death of Jesus our Savior.

God's Messengers
Patrol the Earth

THERE SEEMS LITTLE doubt that this last vision is intended as a parallel to the first in chapter 1. Yet despite the similarities there are significant differences. In both there are horses (in one case with chariots) patrolling the earth, but not all the details correspond. In the first vision they have returned from patrolling the earth to announce that all is at peace; in the second they are eager to set out on their divinely appointed task.

Victory Secured

THERE IS A dreamlike incompleteness to this last vision. In a kaleidoscopic way the various elements shift and change. The horses represent the four winds of heaven, yet only three points of the compass are named; the east drops out of view, as also does the red horse. And what do the two bronze mountains symbolize? No explanation is given and we can only surmise that they are related in some way to the two great bronze pillars that stood at the entrance to Solomon's temple (described in 1 Kings 7:15–22), God's earthly dwelling place. Yahweh was associated with mountains, first with Mount Sinai in the making of the covenant, and then with Mount Zion, his holy city. But whatever the uncertainties of interpretation, there is no doubt that this, the last of the visions, ends on a victorious note. As one commentator writes, "It is as though we have been brought to the last act of a play in which all the tensions and conflicts have been resolved" (R. Mason, *The Books of Haggai, Zechariah and Malachi*). This is confidence grounded not in human reason but in faith in the living God.

As in several of the previous visions, there is a conversation between the prophet and the interpreting angel. The four winds, or "spirits," of heaven, so the angel explains, are setting out on their mission of patrolling the earth after "presenting themselves before the Lord of all the earth." There is an allusion here to the "heavenly council," an idea that occurs a number of times in the Old Testament. The best-known example is found in the first two chapters of the book of Job, where the heavenly beings, the Satan ("Adversary") among them, present themselves before the Lord.

Zechariah's visions speak primarily to the imagination. Their visual impact challenges us with the mystery and "otherness" of God, who works in and beyond history. The Old Testament never allows us to forget that the God who is close to us and always ready to hear our prayers is no mere superhuman but wholly other than his creation. This is why it associates his presence at the giving of the law on Mount Sinai with thunder, fire, and smoke (Exodus 19:16–18) and at the dedication of Solomon's temple with cloud and darkness (1 Kings 8:10–13). Yet the mystery unfolded in the Gospels is greater still, for this Almighty God, creator of all that is, seen and unseen, has entered our world in its suffering and sin, a mystery beyond human understanding.

When we quiet our restless minds and contemplate the mystery of divine love and mercy, all we can do is worship and adore. And what better words can we use than the exclamation of Paul the apostle:

O the depth of the riches and wisdom and knowledge of God!
How unsearchable are his judgments and how inscrutable his ways!
ROMANS 11:33

PRAYER
Lord, when we find the scriptures difficult to understand, give us the faith
which trusts, not in our own finite understanding,
but in your infinite love.

A Symbolic Crowning

THE STRANGE VISIONARY experiences are over and Zechariah seems now to be concerned with a practical matter, the making of a crown for Joshua the high priest. But the passage is not quite as straightforward as the opening sentence might lead us to believe. This "coronation" is a symbolic action and its significance reaches beyond the immediate to give a hint of God's coming kingdom and the Messiah. Symbolic actions were characteristic of some of the prophets, not merely as illustrations of their spoken word but powerful as messages in their own right. Jeremiah for a time wore a wooden yoke over his shoulders symbolic of the imminent fall of Jerusalem, and Ezekiel performed a number of even stranger actions.

The Messiah Promised

THE PASSAGE AS it stands is enigmatic. Whether this was its original form or whether it is the result of development at a later time is uncertain. One thing seems clear—Joshua the high priest is to be crowned. But are there two crowns or one (the Hebrew word is plural) and was Zerubbabel's name once included? Now only an unnamed, shadowy figure appears, identified as the Branch, a title used in the Old Testament of the coming Messiah of David's line. At first the context suggests that Zechariah is thinking of Zerubbabel who, as we have already seen, was prominent in rebuilding the temple. But the prophet's words have a deeper significance, pointing on to a yet unnamed future Messiah who "shall sit and rule on his throne" (v. 13), a hope that in Zerubbabel's lifetime would have been regarded as open rebellion against Persian rule. A strange silence surrounds Zerubbabel, who, after his prominence in the book of Haggai, now fades from view. The emphasis on Joshua, on the other hand, accords with the historical fact that in Israel after the Exile the high priests came to prominence as the civil as well as religious leaders. But the expectation of a kingly Messiah persisted through the centuries, until for Christians it was fulfilled in Jesus' coming.

Conflicts between kings and priests had marked Israel's history from time to time. But in the new age there will be harmony, a "peaceful understanding between the two of them." We are reminded of the two olive trees in chapter 4.

A Broader Vision

IN ZECHARIAH'S TIME, the late sixth century B.C., the rebuilding of the Jerusalem temple was a priority, at least among certain segments of the population. But the close of this passage speaks enigmatically of a future time and a nonmaterial temple when "those who are far off shall come and help to build the temple of the Lord" (v. 15). This is not so much a reference to other exiles who are yet to return (though that may be part of its meaning), as a hint at God's welcome of all, of whatever nation, into his kingdom. It is a mistake to limit the prophet's words to the literal and the immediate. Behind them lie glimpses of yet greater things, more all-embracing hopes than the prophet himself could recognize.

The message of Zechariah contained in chapters 1–8 began with a sharp challenge to repentance. It rises to a climax here with a call to obedience. The privilege of receiving God's promises brings an obligation on those who hear. Zechariah's audience were faced with a choice, to listen or to ignore, to obey or to reject. And so are we who read these words centuries later when the promised Messiah has already come and brought us salvation.

PRAYER

We give thanks today, Lord, for your holy word, for the prophets who looked for the coming of the Messiah, and for the fulfillment of their hopes in the coming of Jesus.

RIGHT PRIORITIES

NOW AT LAST we are on firmer ground once more! We are back in the world of dates and places, the regular currency of history. The year is 518 B.C., two years after the events of chapter 1. Instead of extraordinary visions, we have a plain, straightforward question put to the priests and prophets by a delegation from Bethel, an ancient and famous sanctuary. It was here that Jacob had a notable encounter with God as he dreamed of a ladder set up between earth and heaven, with angels ascending and descending on it. Here was a place of communication between earth and heaven, and that was why Jacob gave the place the name Bethel, "the house of God." In later times, when the kingdom split into north and south after Solomon's death, Jeroboam, the first king of the northern kingdom, established a sanctuary at Bethel as a rival to Jerusalem, and there he set up a calf image. It was still in Zechariah's time a name to be reckoned with.

It was part of the priests' role, in addition to their sacrificial duties, to give authoritative answers on legal matters, as we saw from the book of Haggai. And this was the question that the delegation brought: Now that the Exile was over and the temple already in process of restoration, were they still to keep the days of fasting and mourning they had observed so scrupulously in the fifth month during the past years? This particular fast commemorated the destruction of Jerusalem and the temple (you will find the account of this in 2 Kings 25:8–9). It was not surprising, then, when the temple was being rebuilt, that this particular question should arise. They had no wish to incur the divine displeasure by seeming to ignore the fast through apathy or indifference. And so they came to seek the Lord's favor and to request his guidance.

A Sermon

ZECHARIAH'S RESPONSE WAS surprising. In place of a plain answer and clear guidance (the answer in fact doesn't come until 8:18–19) the prophet launches into a rebuke, in tone not altogether unlike the beginning of chapter 1. It is in effect a sermon, and not just for the delegation from Bethel but "for all the people of the land *and the priests.*" The latter were clearly not in a position at this juncture to give guidance to others. They, too, were open to rebuke. No wonder the prophet had to assume what would normally have been their responsibility. Zechariah doesn't pussy-foot; his challenge is an uncomfortable one for his audience, and for us as well, digging deep into our motivation. The community had carefully observed the fasts, and those of the seventh month too—possibly a reference to the Day of Atonement, or alternatively to the assassination of Gedaliah, governor of Judah after the fall of Jerusalem (2 Kings 25:25). It was their motives that were at fault. The words in Hebrew are emphatic: "Did you fast for me, even me?" God asks. And when, on non-fast days, they ate and drank, was their commitment to him any better? Zechariah underlines the authority of his message with reference to his predecessors, prophets like Isaiah and Amos in pre-exilic times when Jerusalem was prosperous, before the city fell to Babylon in 587 B.C. They, too, had emphasized that ritual without commitment was unacceptable to God.

Read prayerfully what Isaiah 58:6–9 says on the subject of fasting and notice the promise with which it ends:

Then you shall call, and the Lord will answer;
you shall cry for help, and he will say, Here I am.

PRAYER

Lord, in your mercy, search our hearts and purify our motives. Grant that all we do may be done for you and for your glory.

LESSONS FROM HISTORY

ZECHARIAH'S SERMON WAS hard-hitting, but he had not yet finished with his congregation. There was still more "food for thought." And so here is a second sermon, another lesson from history. He begins on a positive note: What God requires is not the externals of worship but commitment demonstrated in daily life, in justice, kindness, and mercy, in care for the disadvantaged and the poor. (Isn't there a modern ring to these words?) This was no new message. Prophets down the centuries, such as Isaiah, Amos, and Hosea, had spoken of a God who loves compassion and justice. Worship must express itself in life. To put it in New Testament terms, "the command that Christ has given us is this: Whoever loves God must love his brother [and sister] also" (1 John 4:21, GNB).

Given in Trust

THERE IS AN enormous difference between ancient Israelite society and modern-day communities, in the prosperous West at least. Our life expectancy, our medical "miracles," and our high technology are some of the more obvious contrasts. Yet some things do not change. There are still many on the margins of society who have been left behind by the growth in affluence. And always there is the temptation for those with comfortable lives to look inward, forgetting to care and to share. What God has endowed us with is given in trust, whether it be financial means, talents, or time. It is for his disposal, an offering to be surrendered to him in worship. We may have little time at our disposal or few resources, but God holds us accountable for what we have, not for what we do not possess.

Zechariah's audience couldn't plead ignorance of God's will. Down the generations Israel had refused to listen; they "turned a stubborn shoulder" (so says the Hebrew in verse 11). In that largely agricultural society no one could have misunderstood what the prophet meant. They knew too well what it was to struggle with a stubborn ox or mule!

Zechariah looks back to his people's recent past, to the years of exile still fresh in their memory. It was too easy to suppose that God had been unable to save his people from Babylon's might. Not so! says Zechariah. God is Lord of history: "*I* scattered them . . ." (v. 14). And God, who has power to scatter, has also power to gather and to remake.

There is no neutrality in our relationships with God; we are either for or against him. Zechariah's sermon ends on a sad note—the people were cut off by their own choice from the God who delights to answer prayer and "a pleasant land was made desolate." Thankfully there is more to follow. The next chapter redresses the balance, for God loves to forgive.

To Think Over

SIN BRINGS PUNISHMENT, says Zechariah; wrong choices have their repercussions. But suffering is not *proof* of sin, as Job discovered. The innocent often suffer because of the guilty.

PRAYER
*Lord, give us the wisdom to choose what is right and the
will to do it day by day.*

A Broken Relationship Restored

ZECHARIAH'S SERMON ENDED on a negative note, but now there are words of hope. There is always a future and a promise for those who trust the Lord. The best is yet to be.

We meet again that word "jealous" that came first in 1:14. It speaks of God's passionate commitment to his people and his concern for their welfare, but this necessarily has two aspects: anger against all that is evil, and its converse, overflowing blessing. The Good News Bible explains the concept: "I have longed to help Jerusalem because of my deep love for her people, a love that has made me angry with her enemies" (v. 2), but to be true to Zechariah and the other prophets we have to add, "and with Jerusalem, too, for her stubborn refusal to listen."

A New Name

AFTER ALL ITS past corruption, its desolation, and despair, Jerusalem will be transformed by the presence of the living God. A change of status is commonly marked by a change of name, and this is no less true of the Bible than of societies ancient and modern. Jerusalem is to be renamed "the faithful city" and Zion "the holy mountain." God holds no grudges. He is ready to start again, the past forgiven. A few years before Zechariah another prophet had put it like this, in Isaiah 62:4:

> *You shall no more be termed Forsaken,*
> *and your land shall no more be termed Desolate;*
> *but you shall be called My Delight Is In Her (Hephzibah)*
> *and your land Married (Beulah).*

God's presence at the heart of a community brings transformation. Instead of "a pleasant land made desolate" there is the vision of a joyful city, its blessings measured not by the wealth of its citizens, by the success of its business life, or by the blossoming of its art and culture, but by the contentment of its aged and the laughter of its children. The prophet sees beyond the present into a more glorious future. Here is true security; the vulnerable live their lives in peace, sitting in the streets, playing in the streets, no need to hide away in fear. Doesn't this conjure up in our minds TV's recurrent images of deserted, empty streets in war-torn countries, silence where happy children should be at play? "Thy kingdom come," we pray.

Don't Limit the Lord

DOES A TRANSFORMATION like this, a new beginning, seem impossible to you? asks Zechariah of his hearers. "Should it also seem impossible to me? says the Lord of hosts." Perhaps this conversation reminds you of that other one between Jesus and the anxious father worried about his son. "All things can be done for the one who believes," said Jesus. And the boy's father immediately cried out, "I believe; help my unbelief!" (Mark 9:23, 24) Nothing is more preposterous than to seek to measure God's power by our own understanding.

For Zechariah, Jerusalem has become more than an earthly city. It stands as a symbol of God's all-embracing kingdom, his people gathered from east and west and brought safely home. Ezekiel before him had spoken of a new Jerusalem. Indeed, the final words of Ezekiel's long book spell out a new name for God's holy city, "The LORD is There" (*YHWH shammah*). Our passage in Zechariah ends on a deeply personal note: "They shall be my people, and I will be their God, in truth and justice" (v. 8, NEB). The relationship sealed by covenant at Mount Sinai, with which Israel's life as a nation began, is restored.

PRAYER

Lord, grant us a wider vision which reaches beyond our own resources of knowledge, strength, or love, and help our unbelief.

LIVING THE LIFE OF GOD'S KINGDOM

THE PREVIOUS VERSES were filled with the promise of God's coming kingdom and its attendant blessings. God offered his gifts, new hope and new life, expressed in worldly terms yet far transcending the normal experiences of life. But people are not robots. They have a part to play and are called to cooperate with God in preparing for the coming of his kingdom.

So, says Zechariah, you need courage, that confidence in God that knows that the future is in his hands. There are many different ways of expressing this in English, and it is interesting to look at more than one translation. "Take heart," says the REB; "Have courage!" says the Good News Bible. The Hebrew expression is more practical, it denotes action: "Let your hands be strong" (so the NRSV). Zechariah isn't talking merely about feelings. He is urging his hearers to take action, to respond to what God has promised. In his two previous sermons (chs. 1 and 7) Zechariah referred to prophets of long ago. Now he reminds them of what they had heard from Haggai not long before.

Worship's Public Face

THE REBUILDING OF the temple has been a turning point, a potent symbol of renewed commitment to God, publicly establishing worship at the heart of the community. As we saw earlier, sometimes these later prophets, such as Haggai, Zechariah, and Malachi, are compared adversely with earlier ones for laying too much emphasis on the rebuilding of the temple and the externals of religion. But at the heart of this emphasis lay devotion to God and its public expression within the community. Individual commitment matters, and so do personal, private devotions. But worship must have a public face and so, too, must commitment if it is to undergird society and shape its values, and thus gather others into the family of God.

Zechariah's words reflect the problems of his time, the poverty and unemployment of the early years after the return from exile, the fragmentation of society with people at odds with each other. But God is the God of new beginnings. Instead of a negative witness to the world around, Israel will be a blessing, a testimony to what God can do, only "do not be afraid, but let your hands be strong" (v. 13). Zechariah is not afraid to repeat what he has just said. He knows how quickly sermons are forgotten!

And why should they (or we) be afraid? God has promised, "I will save you" (v. 13). But now for our part of the task: "These are the things that you shall do" (v. 16, RSV). Not only is courage needed; there is to be obedience too. Here is God's checklist for private and public behavior! "Speak the truth to each other and make sure that the courts administer justice." And, lest there should be any mistake, Zechariah rubs it in—no evil scheming, no perjury. These are not options for God's people then or now: "All these are things that I *hate.*" Strong words, underlined by a most solemn declaration; this is no less than an "oracle of the Lord."

Once again we find that these ancient words, more than twenty-five centuries old, are relevant to our modern world. But are those great ideals—truth, justice, and harmony—any nearer to fulfillment now than they were in Zechariah's time?

MEDITATION AND PRAYER
Read Psalm 24:

Who shall ascend the hill of the Lord?
And who shall stand in his holy place?
Those who have clean hands and a pure heart,
who do not lift up their souls to what is false,
and do not swear deceitfully.

PSALM 24:3–4

Day by day, grant us, Lord, the courage to seek your will and the
strength to live by it.

UNLIMITED BLESSINGS

HERE IS ZECHARIAH'S final word, a picture of total joy and blessing, of harmony among nations bound together by their common purpose of seeking the Lord. And at last Zechariah answers the question put to him in 7:3, broadening it out to include all fasting. Because of God's saving action, all the sad days of mourning that commemorated the fall of Judah and Jerusalem, and other tragedies in the nation's life, will be transformed into joyful festivity. But that does not mean an end to obeying God's will. *Because* God has transformed sorrow into gladness, *therefore,* says Zechariah, you must love truth and peace. Blessing brings responsibility and God's free gift deserves thankful obedience.

Room for All Nations

BUT ZECHARIAH DOESN'T end there. Still more and wider blessing is to come. There is room here for many nations. The last paragraph is a grand description of the power of personal and corporate testimony. The inhabitants of one city say to another, "Come with us. We're going to seek the Lord. I myself am going." Here is testimony by word, reinforced by action. These citizens mean business. They are demonstrating their commitment to God. Imagine the scene—nations coverging on God's city, united in their desire to worship the one and only God, dimly shadowed perhaps today in the thousands from many lands who flock to Jerusalem, not as tourists but as pilgrims to follow in Jesus' footsteps. Zechariah's picture reminds us of that "multitude that no one could count, from every nation . . . standing before the throne and before the Lamb" (Revelation 7:9).

Personal Testimony

ZECHARIAH'S WORDS BECOME more personal, not now the inhabitants of cities but individuals of every language (a reversal of the "Tower of Babel") come to seek the Lord. His description is vivid: Ten foreigners in their eagerness clutch at the clothes of one Judean because, as they say,

"We have heard that God is with you." This is the privilege of the Jewish people, to be the medium of revelation to the Gentiles. And so indeed they were in the birth of Jesus, "a light to lighten the Gentiles and the glory of God's people Israel"; our Immanuel, "God with us."

Two strands have intermingled in Zechariah's message: The practical concern for his contemporaries stands alongside the larger vision of God's coming kingdom. Practical and visionary elements are interwoven. And so Zechariah shall have the last word in this part of our study. Not by accident do these eight chapters end as they do, refusing to bolster complacency with comfortable words, but instead issuing a powerful challenge: "Let us go with you, for we have heard that God is with you." Is this the impression that we make, that our church makes, on those with whom we come into contact?

Seeing God's Glory

MOSES SAID, "SHOW me your glory, I pray" (Exodus 33:18).

"The Word became flesh and lived among us . . . and we have seen his glory" (John 1:14).

"Did I not tell you that if you believed, you would see the glory of God?" (John 11:40)

PRAYER

Lord, grant that our lives may so reflect your glory that others may seek you and, seeking, be found by you.

PREPARING FOR GOD'S KINGDOM

CHAPTERS 9–11 DIFFER considerably from the earlier part of the book. Their style is different. They lack not only the visions, which are so prominent a part of what precedes, but also any reference to Zechariah himself. Yet this is no random addition to the book. There are themes in common, especially the concern for Jerusalem and, at the same time, the inclusion of other nations within God's purposes. Difficult and often uncongenial though these chapters may be in many instances to modern readers, they had a significant place in shaping early Christian understanding of the person and work of Jesus and are quoted several times in the Gospels.

Zechariah 9:1–8 is an oracle against foreign nations. There are many oracles of this kind in the Old Testament prophets. This one concerns the nations that border Israel's territory: Syria with its capital, Damascus; Phoenicia, a seagoing nation renowned for its wealth and for its two famous cities, Tyre and Sidon; and four of the five great Philistine cities (Gath is omitted, probably destroyed by this time). The name of one of these cities is particularly familiar to us nowadays through the many references in the news to "the Gaza strip." God is spoken of in human terms as a warrior (much as an earlier prophet did in Isaiah 59 and 63) who keeps guard over his people now that he has seen "with (his) own eyes" the oppression that they suffer.

The Lord of All

IT IS EASY for us to misunderstand passages like these and to assume that they are jingoistic, bolstered by the complacent conviction that God is guaranteed to be on Israel's side. But this fails to notice their serious significance. They are, in effect, a courageous affirmation, based on faith, that Yahweh is Lord of all nations, and that evil of every kind, in Israel as much as elsewhere, must be rooted out in preparation for the coming of his kingdom. Does our faith in God's victory match up to that?

Despite some difficulty in interpreting the Hebrew of verse 1 (which accounts for the considerable differences you will notice if you compare several translations), the general meaning of the passage is clear enough. Despite the resources of Tyre and Sidon, their wisdom, their impressive defenses, and vast wealth, "silver like dust, and gold like the dirt of the streets," none of this can purchase salvation or win God's approval. All nations are accountable to God.

Although the use of historical place names suggests that the writer may have had in mind a particular event of history, it is more likely that this is symbolic of Yahweh's ultimate victory. Be that as it may, there is a remarkable statement in verse 7. The Philistines, so often depicted in the pages of the Old Testament as bitter enemies of Israel and mocked as "the uncircumcised Philistines," will be incorporated into God's people, just as the Jebusites were after David had captured their city, Jerusalem—another potent warning to the Jewish people of this late period B.C. that Yahweh's sovereignty extended beyond their borders. Although all stand in need of his cleansing from false worship (this is the significance of the gruesome imagery of verse 7), there is room for all in his mercy.

A THOUGHT

There is no racism, sexism, or ageism with God.

After this I looked, and there was a great multitude that no one could count, from every nation, from all tribes and peoples and languages, standing before the throne and before the Lamb. . . . They will hunger no more, and thirst no more . . . and God will wipe away every tear from their eyes.

REVELATION 7:9, 16–17

SING FOR JOY!

HERE IS A song to gladden our hearts! Picture the scene in your imagination—the cheers and the shouting, the acclamation of the king. At this time Israel had no king. For several centuries it had been under foreign rule. But the vision of a coming king, God's Messiah, still held, just as in the passages we read from Isaiah 9 and 11 at Christmastime. The tone of this passage is not so much a longing for the future as the certainty of faith, which looks beyond the present moment to a greater reality of God's making.

The Servant King

THIS PASSAGE IN Zechariah depicts an unmistakably kingly figure, not walking but riding into his capital city. And he comes in triumph, "his cause won, his victory gained, humble, and mounted on a donkey" and, with the parallelism characteristic of Hebrew poetry, "on a colt, the foal of a donkey" (REB). This is no military leader seated on a powerful charger; he comes to abolish the weapons of war, the chariots and the war-horses, for here is power of a different kind. This is no other than "the Servant King." Years later in Jerusalem, as the Gospels tell us, Jesus acted out this scene, a peace-loving, humble figure riding into his city on a donkey, and a borrowed one at that! The significance of his action would not be lost on the onlookers, for they knew well these ancient scriptures that were read constantly in their synagogues. And they rejoiced at this affirmation that Jesus was God's chosen king, although very soon the shouts of the mob had a different tone: "Crucify him! . . . We have no king but Caesar" (John 19:15, RSV).

Much of Israel's life, then as now, was lived under the threat of war from more powerful nations. It is not surprising, then, to find that a constant feature in visions of the future is the cessation of war. All nations are included in this reign of peace, a universal reign that stretches "from sea to sea and from the River (possibly the Euphrates) to the ends of the earth" (v. 10).

There are many lovely phrases here to repay prayerful meditation: "the blood of my covenant" (referring to the covenant made at Sinai and echoed by Jesus with deeper meaning at the Last Supper), "prisoners of hope" (REB "captives waiting in hope"), "he shall proclaim/speak peace to the nations." But then, in contrast, we feel a sense of disappointment as the passage reverts to militaristic language with its talk of hostilities between Israel and Greece, reflecting perhaps the Hellenistic period that began with the rise of Alexander the Great about 330 B.C. We need to remember that here, as always, the Old Testament is grounded in the real world. It reflects life as Israel encountered it in a rough and brutal world, a world of fear and suffering, where deliverance was hard won by victory over enemies.

MEDITATION

"Love your enemies," said Jesus in the Sermon on the Mount,
"and pray for those who persecute you."

MATTHEW 5:4

Yet there is a triumph in which we should rejoice:

"Death has been swallowed up in victory."
"Where, O death, is your victory?
Where, O death, is your sting?"

. . . Thanks be to God, who gives us the victory through our Lord
Jesus Christ.

1 CORINTHIANS 15:54–55, 57

A VICTORY FEAST

ONCE AGAIN THIS passage is full of contrasts, a picture of light and shadow. Some translations, for example the NRSV, present a truly gruesome, even if metaphorical, scene in verse 15 of victorious Israel devouring those who have attacked them and drinking their blood as freely as if it were wine. But beware! This is one interpretation of a difficult passage and neither "the slingers" nor the "blood drinking" is in the Hebrew text. Rather, it is the picture of a celebratory banquet, of eating and drinking when the fighting is past. We need to pause before we take this passage as evidence with which to condemn the bloodthirsty attitude of the Old Testament. It belongs, as we have seen, in a brutal world where death and destruction were everyday occurrences. It doesn't pussyfoot around and its figurative language is often militaristic and even gruesome. But verse 15 is unexceptionable when translated literally:

> *The Lord of hosts will shield them,*
> *they will eat and trample on the slingstones.*
> *They will drink and make a noise like wine.*

In other words, it will be a boisterous, noisy banquet.

God the Savior

THIS IS UNDENIABLY a picture of the warrior God, but the climax to which it points is verse 16: "On that day the Lord their God will save them . . ." This and the following verse, with their lovely imagery, are a welcome counterbalance to what has gone before. Those he has saved are his "flock," they shine "like the jewels of a crown" (literally, "the stones of a crown," a deliberate contrast to the "slingstones" of the earlier picture), so great is the value God sets on his people, and so glorious the beauty of the redeemed. Here is a reminder that however often Israel turned from God and ignored his mercy, and however often we do likewise, he sets great value on his people. Nowhere is this more evident than in the Gospel's declaration that "God so loved the world that he gave his only son" (John 3:16). But the writer of these verses in Zechariah knows well that the beauty of God's people is a derived beauty, hence his exclamation, "What goodness and beauty are his!" (That is, God's, not the land's, as the Good News Bible suggests.) Old Testament writers, as much as New Testament ones, were overwhelmed as they contemplated the mystery of God's love and mercy, of his provision for our needs. On the whole they expressed this blessing in material terms as in our reading here with its reference to grain and wine, though they were well aware that there were blessings that transcended material ones. One of the finest of these expressions is found in Psalm 73:

Whom have I in heaven but thee?
And there is nothing upon earth
that I desire besides thee.
My flesh and my heart may fail,
but God is the strength of my heart
and my portion forever.
PSALM 73:25–26, RSV

PRAYER
Lord, grant to me such awareness of your presence and such experience of your love that I may be able to make the psalmist's words my own.

SHEEP WITHOUT A SHEPHERD

THE WRITER TURNS abruptly from his vision of future salvation to the present situation. It is as if the glorious picture he has drawn of future blessing, corn and wine in abundance, reminds him of present necessity.

In ancient Israel, harvests depended on the regularity of the seasons. The autumn and spring rains, often referred to in the Bible as the early and latter rains, were essential in order to ensure the growth of crops before the drought and heat of summer. Israel celebrated its annual New Year festival in the autumn, the great Feast of Tabernacles, or Booths, where God was acclaimed as both king and Creator, as we saw in our study of Zephaniah 1:2. It was a harvest festival, thanking God for harvest past and praying for rain for a successful harvest to come. In earlier times, prophets such as Hosea had needed to remind the people that it was Yahweh, not Baal, a Canaanite fertility god, who provided them with nature's bounty. In our present passage the concern is somewhat different, but the heart of the matter is the same. The people are faced with a choice: To whom will they entrust their future? Will they reach out in faith and commit themselves to the Lord, a God whom they cannot see, an act demanding total trust, or will they choose a less demanding way, putting their confidence in fortune-tellers, who profess to reveal the future? The biblical writer is in no doubt. It is the Lord and he alone who holds all things in his hands. The future is known to him alone. It is for us to walk by faith not sight, secure in our loving, living Lord.

> *Peace, perfect peace, our future all unknown,*
> *Jesus we know, and he is on the throne.*
> FROM THE HYMN "PEACE, PERFECT PEACE"
> BY BISHOP E. H. BICKERSTETH, 1875

Fortune-tellers or the Lord?

THE INCLUSION OF "teraphim" among the means of fortune-telling is interesting. In early times teraphim were household gods. Rachel stole the teraphim of her father, Laban, when she fled from home with her husband, Jacob, a story you will find in Genesis 31:19–35. But in this later period they have become a means of supernatural guidance and a way of foretelling the future. Yet all that come from these diviners and dreamers are lies and empty consolation—and unreliable hopes. The people are left to their own devices, leaderless and lost. The prophet's words are poignant:

The people wander like sheep;
they suffer for lack of a shepherd (v. 2).

The links with the New Testament scarcely need pointing out. On the occasion when a great crowd followed Jesus into the desert it was these words from Zechariah that he echoed, describing the people as "like sheep without a shepherd." But he, the good Shepherd, was able to meet their need and he fed the five thousand right there in the desert (Mark 6:34).

Read again the familiar words of John 10:14–15 and rejoice that we are no longer "sheep without a shepherd":

I am the good shepherd. I know my own and my own know me, just
as the Father knows me and I know the Father. And I lay down my
life for the sheep.

PRAYER

Lord, grant us the faith to trust you and the strength to follow you in the
darkness as in the light, knowing that the future is safe
in your loving hands.

THE ORDINARY MADE EXTRAORDINARY

THE THEME OF sheep and shepherd continues from the previous verse but, as often in Old Testament poetry, the image has shifted. The people have just been described as sheep without a shepherd, but now the center of attention is false, untrustworthy shepherds, those leaders who lead their people astray. Since little is known of the background to these words, it is impossible to be sure whether the false shepherds are foreign rulers or leaders within the community. But two thoughts stand out: The Lord cares for his people, and he himself will strengthen them. Instead of being like a leaderless flock, wandering and aimless, he will make them strong and purposeful, a splendid war-horse instead of a lost sheep!

The dominant theme throughout this passage is God's compassion for his people. The message is clear: God not only cares, he transforms and remakes. Even the past with all its sorrow and sin can be undone:

> *I will have compassion on them*
> *and bring them all back home.*
> *They will be as though I had never rejected them.*
> *I am the Lord their God; I will answer their prayers (v. 6).*

This is a passage about the difference that God can make. We move in these few verses from the picture of a straying flock with irresponsible shepherds to a people strong in the Lord, old and young, rejoicing not in their own achievements but exulting "in the Lord." Such is God's promise of blessing. Remember the revolutionary songs of those two women, Hannah in the Old Testament (1 Samuel 2) and Mary in the Gospel (Luke 1), celebrating God, who overturns the world's values, lifting up the lowly and bringing joy to the joyless.

Christ the Cornerstone

IN VERSE 4 God promises his people trustworthy leaders, chosen from their own people, Judah. The images of a "cornerstone" and "tent peg" symbolize security, and the "battle bow" represents defense. These are not common metaphors in the Old Testament, though leaders are occasionally described as "cornerstones" (e.g., Isaiah 19:13). Several times in the New Testament Jesus is described as the "cornerstone" of God's building, "built upon the foundation of the apostles and prophets" (Ephesians 2:20), of which all who believe in Jesus are "living stones."

To Think Over

LIKE THE SONGS of Hannah and Mary, the Christian gospel is a revolutionary message. It overturns the conventions of society, celebrating a Savior of lowly birth whose crown was of thorns and whose throne was a cross. "The stone that the builders rejected has become the cornerstone" (Mark 12:10).

> *A PSALM OF THANKSGIVING*
> *I thank you that you have answered me*
> *and have become my salvation.*
> *The stone that the builders rejected*
> *has become the head of the corner.*
> *This is the Lord's doing;*
> *it is marvelous in our eyes.*
> *This is the day which the Lord has made;*
> *let us rejoice and be glad in it.*
>   PSALM 118:21–24

The Same Yesterday, Today, and Forever

HERE IS A promise full of hope. The same God who saved his people in the past, rescuing them from slavery in Egypt, will once again prove to be their savior and will bring his scattered ones back home.

The Old Testament is never bashful about the language it uses to describe the Almighty. Here is a God who "whistles" (v. 8) to his people to call them home (so the REB, though some English versions are more inhibited; the Hebrew word also means "to hiss"). Yet human though this language is, this God is no mere "superhuman." He is the Lord who, in his compassion, takes the first step toward redeeming his people. The initiative is his. Notice how often the word "I" occurs in this passage: "I will whistle for them . . . I will bring them home . . . I will make them strong." This is a God who saves his people when they are helpless to save themselves, the God who is the same yesterday, today, and forever. And yet his actions are always new!

God of Past and Future

TO DESCRIBE HIS vision of the future the prophet looks back to Israel's early history. His words recall the momentous events of the exodus from Egypt and the crossing of the Red Sea (the "sea of reeds") when Israel first became a nation. But his picture is up-to-date and relevant to his contemporaries. Other countries, too, are named here, to which the Israelites had been scattered. But wherever they are, God's power to deliver is still the same. Even the sea itself, as in the Exodus story, will submit to God's control, says the prophet. Here is a new exodus that ushers in a new age and a transformed people:

"I will make them strong in the Lord,
and they shall walk in his name," says the Lord (v. 12).

The prophet's words are poetry, symbolic not literal. God's power and his will to save are promised us for all time and in every situation, but he is the God of surprises, not limited by our expectations, nor by the past. His answers to our prayers are often unexpected, but they are always loving. He is the unchanging, dependable God.

The ancient promises in the book of Zechariah have been fulfilled for Christians in Christ. His death and resurrection belong to history; there was a real cross, a real tomb. And yet what took place in history in time long past, "under Pontius Pilate," as the creed puts it, shapes our present and our future with an eternal hope, for Christ is alive forevermore and has "authority over death and the world of the dead" (Revelation 1:18, GNB).

MEDITATION
The same, yet ever new!

From the beginning of Revelation . . .
"I am the Alpha and the Omega," says the Lord God, who is and who
was and who is to come, the Almighty (1:8);

. . . to the end of Revelation:
He who sat upon the throne said, "Behold, I make all things new." Also
he said, "Write this, for these words are trustworthy
and true" (21:5, RSV).

DOOM AND GLOOM

THE PASSAGE BEGINS with a short poem, an ironical lament. Lebanon is urged, ". . . throw open your gates so that fire may devour your cedars" (v. 1, REB).

Other famous trees, the cypresses and the oaks of Bashan (a fertile region bordering on Lebanon to the southeast) are called on to wail for the destruction of Lebanon's magnificent forests. But the disaster spreads; others are involved. Shepherds wail at their loss, and lions roar in distress for want of their covert in the luxuriant vegetation of the Jordan valley.

The Bible has many ways of illuminating its message. Here it uses a fable to condemn oppressive leaders. The same theme continues in the allegory that follows. Many attempts have been made to understand the historical situation that lies behind it and to determine the identity of the shepherds (leaders) referred to, but these are questions that cannot be answered, for we have too little information of this kind. The Bible is not primarily a history book, but a word from God, challenging us whoever we are, wherever or whenever we live, to do his will. It is a message for all times and all places.

Ruthless Shepherds

IT DESCRIBES FIRST in horrific detail what it means to be at the mercy of ruthless "shepherds," oppressive leaders, who add a religious veneer to their evil deeds: "Blessed be the Lord, for I have become rich" (v. 5). But the prophet is commissioned to be a true shepherd, a trustworthy leader. We cannot tell whether the leaders who are accused are foreign despots or Israel's own corrupt leaders. Either way, the people are exploited, treated like sheep bought and sold in the marketplace, slaughtered for profit. Though the details are obscure, the general meaning of the allegory is clear: No one cares about the helpless poor.

The image of the shepherd is a familiar one in the Bible, particularly in the Old Testament. The best known of the psalms, the 23rd, rejoices that "the Lord is my shepherd," confident of his care even in "the valley of the shadow of death." Kings and rulers are often described as "shepherds," a reminder that they are agents of God, the great shepherd, and their role is to care for others. Too often they fell short of the ideal, enjoying power for its own sake. Ezekiel, way back in the sixth century B.C., had castigated the leaders of his people as shepherds who neither searched for the lost nor fed the sheep. And so God himself would intervene as shepherd, seeking the lost, bringing back the strays, binding up the injured and strengthening the weak (Ezekiel 34:16).

Despite all the problems of understanding this ancient allegory, it is still today a powerful warning to all in positions of leadership, whether in the church or in society. Bad leaders make sad people! If, on the other hand, we reckon ourselves among the sheep, it is a warning to us too. Pray for our leaders that they may be true to their calling. Power, too, easily corrupts. On the integrity of one may depend the fate of thousands.

PRAYER

Lord, grant to those in positions of leadership the wisdom to know what is right and the will to do it, and to us all the courage to stand firm for truth, justice, and peace as followers of the Prince of Peace.

THE ALLEGORY CONTINUES

THESE VERSES MAKE unpleasant reading. This is the Old Testament at its most obscure and its most judgmental. The closing verses send a shudder down one's spine! The details are difficult to interpret and there is much scholarly debate on the subject. It is clear, however, that the specific historical situation that underlies this passage is being described in the form of an allegory, but what exactly that situation was is now impossible to determine.

Foremost among the unanswerable questions is the problem of the identity of the three shepherds dismissed for incompetence and for hostility to God's chosen shepherd. The two staffs were the standard equipment of a shepherd for the defense and guidance of the flock (compare the "rod and staff" in Psalm 23). Named *Favor* and *Union* (REB), they symbolize what the prophet wanted for his confused and distressed people. Sadly, in his failure to achieve this, symbolically he broke the staffs. The allegory is concerned with God's desire for his people and their rejection of his just and gentle rule. The prophet asks for his wages, and receives thirty shekels, the price of a slave. Rejecting God's shepherd, they get the kind of shepherd they deserve.

Thirty Pieces of Silver

DESPITE THE STERN, even horrifying words of judgment with which this passage is replete, we ought not to shy away from it, and this for two reasons. First, it evokes for Christians powerful reminiscences of the Gospel narrative. In the thirty silver shekels thrown into the treasury we are reminded of Judas the traitor, selling his master for thirty pieces of silver and, too late to undo the wrong he had done, throwing them down in bitter remorse in the temple before hanging himself. Judas had time for second thoughts, but tragically no time for second actions. There was no going back—what he had done he had done. Judas' blood money was not fit to be put into the temple treasury, though that is what he intended when he threw it down in the temple. Instead, it was used to buy a field for the burial of strangers, Gentiles, who died in the holy city, Jerusalem. This is a familiar story from Matthew 27:3–8. The Gospel writer has combined these words from Zechariah with material from Jeremiah (probably 32:6–9) and has attributed it all to the latter.

There is another strong reason for not ignoring this passage despite its uncongenial nature and the fact that its devotional content is not immediately apparent: Without doubt an extremely serious historical incident lies behind it. We ought to pause before condemning it as vengeful and reflect for a moment on recent history, where millions have suffered unimaginable horrors simply through the greed and callous indifference of "worthless shepherds." Our highly technological world is far removed from that of the prophet whose words we are reading, but human nature has changed little. There is still abundant evidence of human inhumanity to other humans. The idea that God will raise up a "worthless shepherd" (v. 16) seems perplexing at first sight. It is, however, a serious warning that, when people deliberately reject good leaders, in their place will rise others more congenial to them—worthless leaders.

The lesson we can draw from this obscure, uncomfortable passage is that failure in leadership is no pardonable fault, no trivial misdemeanor. The horrific curse in the closing verse on the worthless shepherd is a plea for his power to be removed, the eye with which he devised his evil schemes and the arm with which he implemented them to be rendered impotent. For then, and only then, can the victims be freed from fear.

PRAYER

Lord, our Creator and redeemer, have mercy on your world. Show your pity on prisoners and refugees, and all who are in trouble, and finally beat down Satan under our feet, through the power of our risen Lord.

THE FINAL CONFLICT

CHAPTERS 12–14 COMPRISE the third and final section of the book of Zechariah. They contain strange, often shocking symbolism to depict the final cataclysm, the ultimate conflict between God and the powers of this world. Such language is the "stock-in-trade" of apocalyptic writers. The last book of the New Testament, too, makes often gruesome reading with its description of plagues and torments, of conquest and death alongside the glorious scenes of the redeemed in heaven offering worship and praise to their Savior God.

The opening words, "An Oracle," are impressive. They demand attention for what follows, for this is the word of the Lord, a point emphasized again in the next sentence by a particularly solemn Hebrew phrase meaning "utterance of the Lord" *(ne'um YHWH)*. Who is this Lord who commands the reader's attention? He is none other than the Creator of heaven and earth, the one who forms (molds) the human spirit within us, the life-giver to whom we owe our very existence. These words in effect supply a title for the whole of chapters 12–14.

All the powers of earth gather to wage war against Jerusalem. But to attack the city of God is a dangerous enterprise; it proves a poisonous cup, a back-breaking stone. Panic and blindness afflict the hostile armies. The picture draws on motifs familiar elsewhere in the Old Testament—the attack of blindness in the Elisha story of 2 Kings 6:18, the panic envisaged in Psalm 48:5–6 of those who would destroy Zion.

Some details of the battle are less than clear. Are the rural inhabitants of Judah for or against Jerusalem at the start? Translations differ. But God promises, "On the house of Judah I will keep a watchful eye" (v. 4). A literal translation of the Hebrew gives the quaint but expressive phrase, "Upon Judah I will open my eyes." In the end it will be acknowledged that "the inhabitants of Jerusalem have strength through the Lord of hosts, their God" (v. 5).

The Weak Made Strong

DESPITE THE HIGHLY figurative language, a brief glimpse of actual history breaks through. There is a hint of tension between urban Jerusalem and rural Judah. But the one who brings salvation also loves equality, and Judah is given a place of honor alongside Jerusalem. The rural areas will share the glory of the city, the weak will be made strong as David was (in his unequal fight against Goliath), and David's royal house, from which the Messiah will come, will lead them in triumph (as God led them in the past on their desert journey).

Zechariah's strange apocalyptic picture is the background to the New Testament protrayal of the "battle of Armageddon" in Revelation 16:16. The language there, with its talk of angels pouring out their bowls of wrath on the earth, is even stranger than Zechariah's. It points, as the apocalyptic writers do, to mysteries beyond this world, in the certainty that in the end God will triumph over demonic evil. But God's victory takes place also within history, in the midst of ordinary human life. And so it was that one day, outside Jerusalem, not by force of arms but through pain and death, a strange victory was won:

He hell in hell laid low,
made sin, he sin o'erthrew,
bowed to the grave, destroyed it so,
and death by dying slew.

FROM THE HYMN
"HIS BE THE VICTOR'S NAME"
BY S. W. GRUNDY, 1838

PRAYER

Lord, in the midst of life's uncertainties give us sure confidence in
Christ's victory won for us, and move our hearts by the power of his love.

NOT REFORMATION BUT TRANSFORMATION

THE PICTURE CHANGES abruptly. Not now an account of battle with all its horrors, but an inner transformation of God's people. The defeat of evil is the necessary converse of his saving love. He pours out a new spirit on his people, "the spirit of mercy and the spirit of prayer," as the Good News Bible puts it. This is not reformation, the people's will to change themselves, but God's doing, his free gift. Here is no "justification by works," no reward given according to merit, but God's loving transformation of what is wrong and unworthy in his people.

The Way of Suffering

OUR ATTENTION IS gripped by what follows. Who is this "one whom they have pierced"? Christians, remembering how John quotes this verse in connection with Christ's death (John 19:37), have no doubt as to the ultimate answer. But here in Zechariah the wounded one is not identified. Like the suffering servant of Isaiah 53, his identity remains a mystery. Is it perhaps the nation, which has betrayed its God-given calling and suffered the consequences? Or is it those country people of Judah, despised as provincial by the wealthier citizens of Jerusalem, who gave their lives for the city's deliverance, as our last passage hinted? It is an unnamed individual who has suffered through the nation's greed and arrogance? Or is it a Messiah yet to come, a vision of what is yet to be? Whichever it is, the significance is clear: Salvation is costly; it involves suffering. But the day will come when those who in ignorance wounded the suffering one will understand and weep.

Everyone is included here in the promise of the outpouring of this "new spirit," the royal house of David, the prophets represented by Nathan, the priestly descendants of Levi. The inclusion of the name Shimei is less obvious. It may refer to Levi's grandson of that name (Numbers 3:18) or to Shimei, a counselor associated with Nathan in supporting Solomon's claim to the throne (1 Kings 1:8). Women have a part equally with men, just as they did on the day of the great outpouring of the Spirit at Pentecost. The details that are given, the separation of families and of wives and husbands in their mourning, probably represents an ancient ritual familiar to the early readers of these verses, as does the reference to the god Hadad Rimmon (possibly signifying "Thunderer") for whom mourning rites were evidently practiced in the plain of Megiddo. No god of this name is mentioned elsewhere in the Old Testament, and it may possibly be a local name for the Canaanite god, Baal. The people will be humbled, recognizing that their deliverance has meant suffering for another, and for this one they mourn.

This passage, like many others in the Old Testament, brings us close to the Christian gospel. For this ancient writer knows that God's gracious gift, which transforms his people, is the *cause*, not the result, of their repentance. And their weeping? This is the *result*, not the cause, of their redemption, for that is God's gift and entirely his initiative.

This passage in Zechariah, for all its difficulty, deserves our prayerful meditation. How much more, then, does the one whose side was pierced on the cross, the sinless for the sake of sinners, deserve our adoration and devotion?

PRAYER

Lord, by the stripes which wounded thee,
From death's dread sting thy servants free,
That we may live, and sing to thee,
Alleluia!

FROM THE HYMN "THE STRIFE IS O'ER," TRANSLATED FROM
THE SEVENTEENTH-CENTURY LATIN
BY THE REVEREND F. POTTS, 1859

BREAKING WITH THE PAST

PROMISE IS HEAPED upon promise for Jerusalem, this time not security from external danger but a radical change bringing spiritual cleansing, a glorious yet humbling promise. "How blessed are those who know their need of God (the poor in spirit)," says Matthew 5:3 (NEB), for pride never avails itself of what God offers. The regrets and weeping of the previous chapter are not sufficient to undo the past. Only God can cleanse and save. He offers a fountain, not clogged by debris and decay but free-flowing and open, always available.

From beginning to end, the Bible makes much of the symbolism of water for cleansing and for life. In its first pages a river flows in God's garden of Eden (Genesis 2:10); on its last page "the river of the water of life" flows from God's throne and brings healing to the nations (Revelation 22:1–2). The Old Testament, like the New Testament, is aware that salvation in its deepest sense is achieved not by human effort (reformation) but solely by God's grace (transformation). Humanity cannot save itself.

Root and Branch Renewal!

BUT EVERY NEW beginning has its cost. Its price is a break with the past, in this case with idol worship. God promises to root out the very names of the idols, to obliterate their memory as truly as if they had never been. This is an offer of total liberation, the gift of freedom to fulfill the first commandment and to worship the Lord alone. But surprise! Along with idol worship, prophets also are included; their spirit is unclean. Long gone were the challenging messages of Isaiah, Amos, and Hosea, and Jeremiah's courageous call for repentance. Even then there had been false prophets whose comforting words confirmed the nation in its headlong rush to disaster. By the later period to which these chapters of Zechariah belong, the prophetic vocation itself had fallen into disrepute. Prophets were no longer the vehicle of God's message.

The Seriousness of Sin

AS OFTEN IN the Bible, we are brought up short. The delightful picture of the fountain that God freely offers his people for their cleansing is followed by a darker scene spelling out the seriousness of sin. The sentiment of verse 3 is horrific, but it underlines both the degenerate state of prophecy, equated with speaking "lies in the name of the Lord," and the accountability of those who infringe God's law. We have to go back to Deuteronomy 13:1–5 to understand the background to these shocking words. We find there a solemn prohibition of making any compromise with prophets who would divert the people from worshiping the Lord:

The Lord your God you shall follow, him alone you shall fear, his commandments you shall keep, his voice you shall obey, him you shall serve, and to him you shall hold fast.

DEUTERONOMY 13:4

The demand in Deuteronomy for total loyalty and unreserved devotion to the Lord is unequivocal. Not even close family ties were accepted as an excuse to acquit those responsible for leading others into apostasy. This is the background to our verse in Zechariah. God must come first. The words are harsh, but the New Testament, too, has its uncomfortable words. Jesus' call to discipleship set the claims of God above all others, including family ties and life itself: "Whoever does not carry the cross and follow me cannot be my disciple" (Luke 14:27).

PRAYER

Lord, we commit ourselves to you for the cause of your glorious kingdom. Keep us loyal and true day by day, living in the light and joy of your presence.

•

THE REPUDIATION OF PROPHETS

THE ATTITUDE TO prophets in this passage comes as a shock! What had once been a high and holy calling had fallen by this time into disrepute. So closely was prophecy now associated with deception that no one any longer dared claim the name of prophet. The visionary experiences associated with prophets and even their traditional garb, the kind of rough garment worn by Elijah, were repudiated. The next time we meet an Elijah-like figure in the Bible, it is John the Baptist. Certainly John's robust, even abrasive call to repentance was poles apart from the comforting platitudes of false prophets.

Denial of a Divine Calling

BY THE TIME of Zechariah 13, the words of Amos many centuries earlier had assumed authoritative status. When the priest of Bethel had accused him of destabilizing the throne of Israel and conspiring against the king, roughly ordering him back to his own country, Amos had denied any hereditary connection with the profession of prophet: "I am no prophet, nor a prophet's son; but I am a herdsman, and a dresser of sycamore trees" (7:14). The disclaimer of this later generation of discredited prophets is modeled on Amos' words. "I am no prophet," they say, "I am a tiller of the soil (literally 'a man serving the soil')." The next few words are puzzling, and you will find that translations vary considerably. Some take the statement as added proof of the credentials of the man concerned: "The land has been my possession since my youth." He has had nothing to do with prophecy but has always been a farmer and nothing else. This interpretation, however, involves making changes in the Hebrew text. Taken literally, the text says, "For man (mankind) has possessed me from my youth." This is perhaps a way for the speaker to distance himself intentionally from those prophets who claimed divine control of their lives. He denies any superhuman commission whatsoever. The contrast with Amos is stark. Although Amos denied being a professional prophet or a member of a prophetic guild, he testified courageously to the hostile priest that the Lord had called him and had given him a divine commission to prophesy (Amos 7:15).

It is tempting for Christians to see a reference to Christ and his sufferings in verse 6, for it was a "friend," Judas the disciple, who betrayed him to those who crucified him. Yet it is worth noticing that although there are several allusions to the book of Zechariah in the gospel narratives, this is not one of them. The wounds mentioned here are literally "between your hands," that is on the back or the chest. Probably in this context the expression refers to the practice of self-mutilation by prophets as in the story of Elijah's encounter with the prophets of Baal on Mount Carmel (1 Kings 18:28). Hosea, too, found it necessary to warn the people that practices such as this were not an acceptable way of approaching God (Hosea 7:14). Now, at this later period, such was the disrepute into which prophecy had fallen that excuses were made for such marks of self-inflicted violence. These wounds, they say, have nothing to do with ecstatic worship; they were simply the result of a brawl in a friend's house. What a sad story of the decline of that once holy vocation!

PRAYER

Lord, you have called us to be messengers of your gospel. Grant that we may never treat lightly our vocation, but be your true and faithful witnesses to our lives' end.

A NEW RELATIONSHIP
FORGED BY SUFFERING

THE STYLE CHANGES from prose to poetry, a reminder that the language of these verses is symbolic, not literal. This is a picture of both light and shade; the dark horror of its opening lines throws into glorious relief the divine promise with which it ends.

At first sight it is one of those passages that shock us with the vehemence of the judgment depicted. However, two things must be borne in mind as we read and meditate on these verses. First, remember the warning in verse 3 that no tolerance is to be shown to those who lead God's people astray, however near and dear they are. Just so, God himself calls down judgment on the leader of his people, although near and dear to him. The identity of this unnamed person is left deliberately vague. We know only that God calls him "my shepherd . . . the man who is close to me" (v. 7, NIV). Whether he suffers for his own sins or for the sins of others we cannot tell. In the New Testament this vague, unidentified figure is brought into sharper focus. There is no mistaking now the identity of God's shepherd: It is Jesus.

Sin and Redemption

YET THIS IS no tyrannical, unpredictable God dealing out arbitrary threats and punishments. This is a God who delights in mercy and whose ultimate purpose is redemption. And so the second fact to bear in mind is this: Although the poem emphasizes the utter seriousness of sin, the folly of rejecting the sovereign Lord, yet it speaks of hope, for there is a "remnant" as Isaiah would have called it. Here is not only punishment that destroys but refining that purifies, for even those who are saved from judgment fall short of God's requirements.

The imagery of silver refined and gold assayed suggests not simply the need for purifying but also how precious this "remnant" is to God, how great the value he sets upon his people. And so the poem ends with a glorious promise for all who trust him:

> *They will call on my name*
> *and I will answer them;*
> *I will say, "They are my people,"*
> *and they will say, "The Lord is our God!" (v. 9).*

The New Testament contains several echoes of this poem. This is a warning to us not to write off as unimportant these short prophetic books at the end of the Old Testament. Sadly, they are rarely read and their common designation as "minor prophets" adds to the perception of them as insignificant. But Jesus knew this passage well and applied it to his own suffering and death. On the way to Gethsemane he warned his disciples as the storm clouds gathered: "You will all become deserters; for it is written, 'I will strike the shepherd, and the sheep will be scattered'" (Mark 14:27).

This shepherd suffered not for any failure on his part but as the innocent for the guilty, a reminder of the new dimension the gospel gives to some Old Testament sayings.

The chapter started with "names"—the names of the idols obliterated from memory (v. 2). It ends with God's name (v. 9). Prayer offered in that name is promised an answer.

FOR MEDITATION
Notice how important in many psalms is the name of the Lord.
Two examples are given here.

Praise . . .
Blessed be the name of the Lord
from this time on and forevermore.
From the rising of the sun to its setting
the name of the Lord is to be praised.
PSALM 113:2–3

. . . and promise:
Our help is in the name of the Lord,
who made heaven and earth.
PSALM 124:8

THE LAST BATTLE

THIS CHAPTER MAKES strange reading until we recognize what kind of writing it is. It differs from the prophets and belongs to the category known as apocalyptic literaure (see Introduction), which speaks in ultimate and universal terms of what is beyond history and outside this world's experience. It depicts in symbolic language the last battle between God and evil, and God's final victory. The closest parallels in the Bible to this kind of apocalyptic writing are Mark 13 and the book of Revelation, but it was a type of literature that flourished in the centuries between the end of the Old Testament and the beginning of the New.

In contrast to chapter 12, where Jerusalem escaped capture, in these verses Jerusalem is plundered and its citizens suffer. The details are realistic, based on familiar battle scenes, but this is not a historical event. It is the ultimate battle in which the world's nations pit their might against the city of God. Despite the suffering, victory is assured, for there is another participant in the battle, the Lord. And now historical scenes are discarded and symbolism takes over. Many times, in psalms and prophets, the Old Testament depicts the Lord's awesome presence, shaking the earth and shattering, sometimes melting, the mountains. We had an example in Habakkuk 3:6 (you may wish to see Micah 1:4 too). It was a way of expressing Israel's awareness of God's transcendent presence, his unearthly grandeur and glory, even though he was like a father to his people, sharing in their sorrows and their joys.

This is the first time the Bible refers to the Mount of Olives by name. Here is a cataclysmic scene, the splitting of the mountain to make a way of escape for God's tormented people. By way of illustration they are reminded of a notable earthquake centuries before in King Uzziah's time. It was two years before that earthquake, in the eighth century B.C., that Amos the prophet was at work (Amos 1:1). But here, as in the book of Revelation, God and his angels prepare for battle.

The language used here differs immensely from the lovely words of

Isaiah 40:4, "Every valley shall be lifted up and every mountain and hill be made low," but the thought is comparable. There the Lord's highway was being prepared for the return of his exiled people; here it is a way of escape for his suffering ones. But what a sad contrast it is to the lovely picture of Jerusalem in Zechariah 2:4–5, a city without walls, open to a vast multitude, protected by the Lord, who is himself its defense and its glory!

A Prelude to the Gospel

THIS LAST CHAPTER of Zechariah is an anthology. Images come and go as in a kaleidoscope. Horrors are intermingled with pictures of a glorious future. But this is the realism that is characteristic of the Bible. The coming of God's kingdom is not an easy, comfortable progress. Evil is a reality, and its defeat is costly. The battle, too, of which the Gospels tell, the ultimate triumph over evil, is a costly one, not couched in terms of the clash of armies, but of a lone individual wrestling on that same Mount of Olives until his sweat became, as it were, great drops of blood falling down to the ground. But victory was won and the final cry of triumph sounded from the cross, "It is finished." Such was the cost of defeating sin and death, a story of horror and of glory. To the gospel of Jesus' victory these verses in Zechariah are merely a prelude, a dim prefiguring of what took place in history and opened for us the gateway to eternal life.

PRAYER
Lord, for your defeat of the powers of darkness, for life and liberty and light, we give you thanks.

A GLORIOUS FUTURE

IT SEEMS AS if all the hopes and longings of the past are gathered here into the picture of a glorious future. Israel had known a long line of kings who failed to live up to their high and sacred office, and long years served under foreign domination. Little wonder that they looked forward to the reign of God, celebrated so often in the psalms as a kingdom of justice and peace.

God's kingdom is not one among many; it is unique and all is new. That is the thought behind these verses. The familiar world of history has gone. These hopes belong to the age to come. The words are reminiscent of God's ancient promise to Noah after the flood:

> *As long as the earth endures,*
> *seedtime and harvest, cold and heat,*
> *summer and winter, day and night, shall not cease.*
> GENESIS 8:22

But in God's glorious coming kingdom, says this apocalyptic writer, the ordinary and the familiar world with its seasons and its transition from day to night will be transformed. The hardships of cold and frost and the dangers, too, of the hours of darkness will be no more. The promise, "at evening time there shall be light," must be seen in the context of the Middle East, where early sunsets are followed rapidly by the onset of darkness.

The New Jerusalem

THE ECHOES OF Psalms 46 and 48 are unmistakable. Although Jerusalem itself has no river, Psalm 46:4 sings in symbolic language of "a river whose streams make glad the city of God."

The writer here in Zechariah takes up that picture: "On that day living waters shall flow out from Jerusalem" to the eastern sea (the Dead Sea) and the western sea (the Mediterranean). Likewise Psalm 48 celebrates the earthly Jerusalem: "[God's] holy mountain, beautiful in elevation, is the joy of all the earth" (v. 2), although, literally speaking, Jerusalem's hill is dwarfed by the mighty peaks of Hermon. That picture, too, is drawn on here in Zechariah in a vision of the future. The symbolic becomes the actual, the surrounding land (though from Geba to Rimmon is a surprisingly small area in contrast to verse 9) becomes a plain, and Jerusalem in solitary splendor stands proud above it. And for God's city there is lasting security. The book of Revelation, too, portrays the new Jerusalem.

"On that day the Lord will be one and his name one" (v. 9). This is a reaffirmation of the great Jewish confession of faith in Deuteronomy 6:4, known as the "Shema" from its opening word "Hear." These famous words are what Jesus recalled when one of the scribes asked him, "Which commandment is the first of all?" Jesus answered, "The first is, 'Hear, O Israel, the Lord our God is the only Lord; you shall love the Lord your God with all your heart, and with all your soul, and with all your mind, and with all your strength' " (Mark 12:29–30).

FOR MEDITATION

Like Zechariah, the New Testament, too, envisages God's new Jerusalem as a city where there is no night, but with one significant difference:

The city has no need of sun or moon to shine on it, for the glory of God is its light, and its lamp is the Lamb.

REVELATION 21:23

THE CONQUEST OF EVIL

THE FIRST PARAGRAPH makes nauseating reading with its horrific portrayal of the grim effects of plague. As we read, we need to bear in mind that the foes depicted in apocalyptic writings were not simply human enemies but the ultimate forces of chaos and evil, in fact the sum total of everything that pits its might against God and plots the destruction of his people. Yet behind this graphic description there probably lies the memory of a historical event. Plague was not unknown in the ancient world and there are reminiscences here of how Jerusalem escaped from the horrors of the siege laid by Sennacherib in 701 B.C. through the onset of a plague (perhaps bubonic) that swept through the Assyrian ranks. Israel's account of this celebrated deliverance is found in 2 Kings 19:32–36.

That isn't, however, the only Old Testament tradition that lies behind this grim description. The prophet draws on the ancient theme of God himself fighting for his people by means of a divinely induced panic that brings chaos to the enemy and turns the hostile forces against each other. A well-known illustration of this tradition occurs in the story of Gideon in Judges 7 when the Midianite troops were thrown into disarray by a motley band equipped only with trumpets, pitchers, and torches, and "the Lord set every man's sword against his fellow" (Judges 7:22). There is a reminiscence, too, of Psalm 48, which describes in nonhistorical cosmic terms an attack by the world's rulers on Jerusalem:

> *See, the kings assemble;*
> *they advance together.*
> *They look, and are astounded;*
> *filled with alarm they panic (vv. 4–5, REB).*

A Threat and a Promise

THEN THE SCENE changes. The fearsome description of plague and pestilence is quickly followed by the assurance that all nations are welcome to join in worship of the king at the yearly Festival of Booths. This was Israel's great pilgrim feast at which they celebrated the Lord as king and Creator (see commentary on Zephaniah 1:2–3). It was a harvest celebration in which they gave thanks for the harvest past and prayed for the rain necessary for the next year's crops, hence the dire fate of those who deliberately ignore the Creator-king, the source of life.

Egypt is a case apart (v. 18), threatened not by lack of rainfall but by plague, because Egypt was not dependent on seasonal rains for its harvests but had its own means of irrigation from the Nile. The difference between Egypt and Israel's promised land is charmingly spelled out in Deuteronomy 11:10–11, the one irrigated "by foot," the other "watered by rain from the sky." But the message of these verses in Zechariah is clear: The Lord is not a God with whom to trifle. Worship is owed to him by all the earth.

Here once again is the challenge that runs throughout the Old Testament, the need to choose for or against the Lord. From the moment in the early chapters of Genesis when Adam and Eve chose their way instead of God's, right through to the last chapter of the book of Revelation, we are called to make a personal choice. The warning at the end of the New Testament of the consequence of rejecting God's word, though not spelled out in detail, is as fearsome as that of Zechariah. But for those who choose to do his will, God's offer is gloriously free:

> Let everyone who is thirsty come.
> Let anyone who wishes take the water of life as a gift.
>   REVELATION 22:17

PRAYER

Lord, give us open ears to hear your word and loving hearts ready to receive your free gift offered in Jesus.

GOD OF THE EVERYDAY

THESE ARE EXTRAORDINARY verses. A radical change is envisaged in the relation between the sacred and the secular, the holy and the profane. This is the end of life as we know it. The familiar seasons, the alternation of light and darkness, are gone, as we saw earlier in the chapter. And now those boundaries between the sacred and the secular that define our approach to God are to be obliterated, not because nothing is holy but because all is holy and acceptable to the Lord.

The vision is spelled out in striking fashion, depicted in such sparse words that meditation and imagination are needed to fill in the picture. What is it that is to bear the inscription "Holy to the Lord"? It is none other than horses, symbolic of war and military might, and symbol, too, of Israel's trust in earthly power. Long before these chapters were written, Isaiah had rebuked the people for a false sense of security in military alliances:

> *Alas for those who go down to Egypt for help*
> *and who rely on horses,*
> *who trust in chariots because they are many*
> *and in horsemen because they are very strong,*
> *but do not look to the Holy One of Israel.*
> ISAIAH 31:1

War itself is abolished. Its animals are consecrated to God, and that in extraordinary terms! For "holy to the Lord" was the inscription on the turban to be worn by the high priest when he ministered in God's presence on the people's behalf.

Radical Change

HERE IS A picture of a people and their possessions offered without reserve to the Lord, consecrated to his service. The sacred has pervaded the profane; the distinction between them, emphasized so forcefully for

Israel in the regulations for the priesthood and for sacrifice, will be eliminated. The ordinary, humble cooking pots of daily living will be holy like the sacred vessels before the altar, for such will be the number of the worshipers that every ordinary domestic cooking pot will be called into service.

Here is radical change, not merely renewal. Materialism and impurity are eliminated. There will be no further need for traders in the temple, buying and selling, exchanging the ordinary items of daily living for what was acceptable in the temple. "There shall no longer be traders in the house of the Lord of hosts," a word fulfilled during the ministry of Jesus. What an extraordinary conclusion to the book, this message of a new age where God is universally acknowledged as king and all nations are included in worship, a vast multitude.

MEDITATION AND PRAYER OF DEDICATION

Because of God's great mercy to us I appeal to you: Offer yourselves as a living sacrifice to God, dedicated to his service and pleasing to him. This is the true worship that you should offer. Do not conform yourselves to the standards of this world, but let God transform you inwardly by a complete change of your mind.

ROMANS 12:1–2, GNB

Lord, all that I have I offer you; all that I am I give to you.

Dishonorable Worship

MALACHI IS UNIQUE in the Old Testament. It is a book full of questions, a book of controversy and argument between the Lord and his people.

Author and Date

UNLIKE THE PROPHETS that precede it, this book appears to be anonymous. "Malachi" in Hebrew means "my messenger" and there is no clear evidence that it was ever used as a proper name. It does, however, fittingly describe the prophet's role. He is indeed the Lord's messenger to bring his word to his people. It is likely that in the absence of the author's name, the term "my messenger" was taken from 3:1 when the book was eventually edited. However, the messenger referred to there is not the prophet.

The date and setting of the message, too, are uncertain. Unlike Haggai and Zechariah, with their very specific dates, there is no date or any clear hint of one given in Malachi. It is generally assigned to the early part of the fifth century B.C. on the grounds that the abuses it criticizes were dealt with by Ezra and Nehemiah, in the reforms they carried out from about the middle of that century. However, our knowledge of the history of this period leaves so many uncertainties that it is difficult to date the book with any precision.

The First Dispute

WHAT AN OUTSPOKEN controversy this is, to the point of bluntness! "I have loved you," says the Lord. But the people are not satisfied. They doubt his love. They want substantial proof. Hosea, many years before, had assured the people that the reason God had rescued them from Egypt was simply because he loved them (Hosea 11:1). But now the people are dispirited. Experience has caused them to mistrust God's love. Their days as an independent nation have gone. The community is impoverished, no longer a proudly independent nation with their own king of David's royal line on the throne. They are part of the Persian Empire under the control of a governor. And so the people retort: Show us the evidence, prove your love!

God's Answer

IN RESPONSE, GOD gives them a twofold proof of how he has intervened on their behalf. The first looks back to past history, to the origins of their nation; the second belongs to recent times. First, there is the ancient story of how Jacob claimed from his elder brother Esau the rights of the first-born, and eventually his blessing. What a trickster he was! Yet despite many doubtful acts, God's care surrounded him and he became the eponymous ancestor of the nation. These fascinating stories are found in Genesis 25:19–34. A more recent disaster, too, had befallen Edom, Esau's descendants. But for Israel, the prophet says, there is a future. God is active.

For Edom the words are harsh, but this is no petty favoritism. Edom was a brother nation turned ruthless enemy at the time of Jerusalem's defeat by the Babylonians (Psalm 137:7). Its name becomes in the Old Testament a symbol of cruel treachery. Moreover, these verses are not purely nationalistic. They affirm that God is powerful even "beyond the borders of Israel." Certainly what follows soon shatters Israel's own complacency. They, too, are accountable for their actions. The privilege of being God's chosen people is no guarantee of an easy future. It can be an uncomfortable calling.

PRAYER

Lord, grant that as we see the evidence of your love in our lives we may be led to humility, not arrogance, and may serve you faithfully as followers of the crucified Lord.

DESPISING THE LORD

FOR THE SECOND time the Lord initiates the dispute. Not Edom but Israel's own priesthood is now the target of the prophet's searing denunciation. The Old Testament is shot through with the demand for respect to be shown to parents and loyalty to masters. So serious in ancient Israel was rebellion against parents that the penalty for the rebellious son who refused to heed warnings or to show remorse was death. The prophet's words, then, are full of challenge. God their father and master, to whom respect and obedience are due, has received neither. He is treated with disdain even by the priests. So far are they sunk in egotism and self-interest, so narrow and materialistic have their horizons become, they feel no shame or fear in despising God. And yet, it seems, this is no deliberate act of rebellion. It is the result of insensitivity, of apathy and indifference, of failure in self-examination. For this reason the challenge to us is the more forceful. Could it be that sometimes we are as insensitive as Israel's priests were to the implications of our actions?

In the very act of worship, the Lord of hosts (twenty-three times Malachi calls him by this awesome title, *YHWH sebaoth*) is belittled and dishonored. But the priests are caught by surprise. They are well satisfied with their actions, their careful observance of ritual. And they are argumentative: "How have we despised your name . . . polluted the altar?" The answer is uncompromising—by substituting grudging obligation for spontaneous, joyful worship. They have given God the leftovers, offering in sacrifice that for which they had no use themselves. Would they dare to make such an offering to their governor? Would it persuade him to show them any favors?

Oh, for an End to Sacrifice!

THE STATEMENT THAT follows (v. 10) must have astounded the prophet's audience. Here is God himself wishing for the temple doors to be closed to put an end to the worship offered there. When set against the background of the psalms with their rapturous celebration of Jerusalem as the city of God where his presence dwells and from which his life-giving water flows, the effect of this charge on the startled hearers can be imagined. Better no offerings at all than unworthy ones. There are times when God will not accept our worship.

The sentiment is similar to Paul's stern words of warning to the Christians at Corinth who were trivializing the Lord's supper: "Examine yourselves," he says, "and only then eat of the bread and drink of the cup" (1 Corinthians 11:28).

Malachi, like the other prophets surveyed here, sometimes seems to be more concerned with religious observance than with social justice, unlike his predecessors before the exile. But he is aware that outward observance is symptomatic of inner commitment, that theology affects daily living and that belief shapes action. The quality of our worship reflects not only the depth of our commitment; it also demonstrates the kind of God in whom, at heart, we believe.

MEDITATION AND PRAYER

Reflect on Psalm 46:1–7 and contrast its joyous certainty of God as "our refuge and strength" with the sad depths to which Malachi's contemporaries had sunk. It is not God who changes. It is the response of the worshipers that makes the difference.

Lord, we confess with shame the times when our worship has become a grudging obligation rather than a spontaneous offering of praise. Lift our spirits and quicken our enthusiasm by the power of your life-giving Spirit, and give us a new vision of your glory, we pray.

THE UNIVERSAL LORD

THE PROPHET TURNS his criticism now on the common people. Their leaders were guilty, but the Old Testament makes it clear that everyone is accountable before God. There is no hiding behind the failures of others.

Verse 11 stands like a beacon of light, throwing into relief the darkness of the accusations that precede and follow it. So negligent are the priests that no offering from their hands is acceptable to God. Yet throughout the wide world there are those who offer "a pure offering" and among whom the Lord's name is great and worthily praised. There has been much debate about the meaning of this extraordinary saying. Some have applied it to faithful Jews scattered throughout the Gentile nations: Others have applied it to Gentile worship wherever this has been sincerely offered. If this is indeed its meaning, and it does seem to be its most obvious sense, it is a welcome counterbalance to the apparent exclusivism of the opening verses of the book, with their emphasis on Israel as the chosen nation. Whatever its original meaning in Malachi's own situation, it is a fitting word to find in the last book of the Old Testament, which points us on to the future, to the new covenant in Christ's death offered to all nations, Gentile as well as Jew.

The Shameful Worshipers

THEN FOLLOWS CRITICISM of the ordinary people and their attitude to worship. They fare no better than their leaders. The criticism is strong: The Lord's table is "polluted," the offerings on it "despised." The worshipers themselves are apathetic. There is no joyful response to God for his goodness, no acknowledgment of his transcendent glory. The full shame of their attitude is well expressed in the Good News Bible with its colloquial translation: "You say, 'How tired we are of all this!' and you turn up your nose at me." Not only is the regulation disregarded that specifies only an unblemished animal as an acceptable offering, but some people have offered to God that which has cost them nothing, in fact that which has been stolen and acquired by violence.

With the last verses of this chapter, Malachi returns to his earlier theme that God's might and majesty transcend the restrictions of one single nation (v. 5). Here his name is revered among the Gentile nations. The utter shame of the worshipers who abuse their privilege and despise their God is underlined in the climax, "I am a great king."

God's Universal Reign

RARELY IN THE Old Testament is God described as simply Israel's king. In general the emphasis is on his universal rule. The psalms that particularly celebrate his kingship (e.g. 93–99) call on all nations, all the earth, to join in worship:

> *Break forth into joyous song and sing praises!*
> *. . . With trumpets and the sound of the horn*
> *make a joyful noise before the King, the Lord!*
> PSALM 98:4, 6, RSV

Not only Israel but also the Gentile nations are included in this call to worship, and not only earth but heaven too, in Psalm 29.

MEDITATION
Give thanks for the glorious promise given to both Jew and Gentile in Ephesians 2:13–14:

Now in Christ Jesus you who once were far off have been brought near by the blood of Christ. For he is our peace; in his flesh he has made both groups into one and has broken down the dividing wall, that is, the hostility between us.

KEEPING FAITH

CHAPTER 1 ACCUSED the priests of dishonoring God. But God does not lightly let his servants go, however unfaithful they are. This chapter calls for a new beginning, "Now, O priests . . ." and it is addressed personally so that there can be no mistaking its target: "This command is for you." Above all, it emphasizes the seriousness of sin and of personal accountability.

A Choice to Make

VERSE 3 SOUNDS horrific to modern ears, but when we see it in context we discover that it has a serious meaning and is not gratuitously offensive. It speaks figuratively of the loss of ritual purity and of subsequent exclusion from priestly office. The choice is their own; it is for them to make on their own account. And it is a solemn one, for to be a member of the priesthood meant both privilege and obligation. It was grounded, says the prophet, in an ancient covenant between God and their forefather, Levi. Malachi, like the book of Deuteronomy, classes priests and Levites together, in contrast to another view in the Old Testament that regards the priesthood as limited to the descendants of Aaron, and the Levites as their assistants. It is God's will that this ancient covenant should hold. But a covenant necessarily has two partners and imposes mutual obligations—the gift of "life and peace" on God's part, matched by the response of reverence on the part of the priests.

Leaders Beware

MALACHI'S VIEW OF priesthood is high. He describes the priest here as "the *messenger* of the Lord of hosts" (v. 7), a role more characteristic elsewhere of the prophets. Malachi is sometimes criticized for the narrowness of his outlook because of his emphasis on sacrifice. This criticism is not entirely justified since it is clear from this present passage that he regards instruction, not sacrifice, as the primary task of the priests. It is the priest who is to "guard knowledge" (v. 7) and to whom the people should be able to come in confidence to seek instruction in God's will. But the priests have betrayed this high calling. The contrast between the ideal and the actual is poignant; the priest's role was to turn "many from iniquity" (v. 6). Malachi may have in mind here the praise heaped upon one of the early priests, Phinehas, in Numbers 25:10–13 because of his utmost commitment to God, by which he rescued Israel from disaster. But the priests of Malachi's time, far from turning others from iniquity, have themselves turned from God's way. True, they have given instruction, but of such a kind that it has "caused many to stumble" (v. 8), a solemn warning today to all who lead or teach. How easy it is to betray our calling, not always deliberately but by negligence or apathy. The greater the calling and the heavier the responsibility, the more urgent is the need for humble watchfulness and self-examination.

PRAYER

Lord, grant your grace to all who lead and teach, that we may humbly commit ourselves to do your will and lay aside all arrogance and self-seeking lest we turn others from your way.

MUTUAL DISLOYALTY

MALACHI TURNS NOW from the priests to the people as a whole. Society is in a sorry state, divided and disloyal when they should have been united by their common history. For they all have one father (Jacob, the ancestor of the twelve tribes of Israel, is meant), and they have one God who created them. And yet they are unfaithful to God and to one another. Two different accusations are made against the community, both linked by the idea of breaking the covenant of marriage. In the first accusation, this is meant metaphorically. They have broken their covenant with God by "marrying" (worshiping) a pagan goddess. For much of its history, Israel was strongly tempted to worship other gods and goddesses whose requirements were less demanding than Yahweh's and whose presence was less mysterious, for they were represented by images that could be seen and handled. But the worship of Yahweh was austere and demanding, and there was no place in it for a goddess. The creation story of Genesis 1 makes it clear that the distinction between the sexes, male and female, belongs to the created order, not to the deity. Yahweh is neither male nor female but transcends gender. Little wonder that the people from time to time turned to Canaanite worship with its inclusion of Asherah, the female counterpart of Baal.

But if their disloyalty to Yahweh showed itself in "marriage" to a pagan goddess, their disloyalty to each other showed itself in divorce, the literal breaking of the marriage bond. The externals of ritual were not neglected. The worshipers wept over Yahweh's altar, knowing that they were estranged. "But why?" they ask. And this is where Malachi's contemporaries, and we, too, are reminded that life cannot be compartmentalized, that worship of Yahweh is not unrelated to the way we conduct our lives each day. The trouble here was unfaithfulness, disregard of promises and vows, not this time made between Yahweh and his people (as in verse 10), but between man and wife. The wives of their youth, those whom they had married in their early days, had now grown old, and there was the temptation to take new and younger wives. But God, who created everyone, man and woman alike, has a purpose for our lives in which divorce has no part, a view similar to that propounded by Jesus in the Gospels.

The failure to keep promises of whatever kind is regarded with the utmost seriousness in the Old Testament. Here surely is a challenge for today's society, both in the public and the private realm. When the question is asked in Psalm 15, "O Lord, who may abide in your tent? Who may dwell on your holy hill?" eleven conditions are set out that involve not only deeds but words and thoughts too. The ninth condition is the following: "[the man] who keeps his oath even when it hurts" (v. 4, NIV). The Good News Bible with its colloquial translation makes the challenge even more pointed: "He always does what he promises, no matter how much it may cost."

What a range of circumstances this covers, from momentous promises to apparently trivial ones. There is no "exception clause" here. But there is a promise for those who do what God requires: "Whoever does these things will always be secure" (v. 5, GNB).

PRAYER
Grant, Lord, that in thought, word, and deed we may be found trustworthy and true, and may be welcomed into your presence in the company of all true worshipers.

GOD'S DAY OF ACTION IS NEAR

CHAPTER 1 DESCRIBED how the priests grumbled and were weary of offering the regular sacrifices. But here it is the Lord himself who is weary, weary of their scepticism, weary of the distortion of his purposes by religious leaders who should have known better. Not only are they asking "Where is God's justice, does he take notice, does he care about human beings? Is he so mighty and we so small that he ignores us?"—the sort of questions that Psalm 73:11 posed when the wicked seemed to prosper: "How can God know? Is there knowledge in the Most High?" Malachi's contemporaries go further than that and malign the very nature of God. The Good News Bible puts it forcefully: "The Lord Almighty thinks all evildoers are good; in fact he likes them" (v. 17). They needed to learn Habakkuk's lesson of patient waiting and trusting. But God answers them. He is going to act decisively—and suddenly. God is sovereign, free to act in his own time and his own way, not constricted by human expectations. Already echoes of the Gospels are awakened, for Jesus, too, spoke of the suddenness of the coming of God's kingdom. So the question now for the priests and people of Malachi's time is no longer "Will God take action, will he come?" but, "Will we be ready for his coming?" And this, too, is a theme of much of Jesus' teaching.

The Herald of His Coming

THE OPENING WORDS of chapter 3 are familiar to us since they are quoted at the beginning of Mark's Gospel. There the messenger is John the Baptist, who prepares the way for the promised Messiah. Here in Malachi, the messenger is less easily identifiable. No name is given nor any hint of whether this is an earthly or a heavenly messenger. In Hebrew the word for messenger (*malach*) can have either meaning. In Oriental society a herald would announce the coming of the king, and this messenger is preparing the way for the Lord of hosts whom Malachi has earlier described as "a great king." This is no cozy coming, no God who guarantees his people's prosperity whatever their spiritual state. Preparation is required of those to whom he comes. The priests must have been shocked by the announcement that God's judgment was to begin with the temple. Again one might protest that Malachi focuses too narrowly on the temple and its sacrificial rituals. But he knows the importance of worship for the well-being of the community and the need for integrity among those who lead the worship and instruct the people. The idea that judgment must begin with God's household is found, too, in the New Testament (1 Peter 4:17). God, who earlier had yearned for the temple doors to be closed that unworthy offerings might be excluded, now speaks of coming "to his temple." Once more it is to be a focus of his worship.

The image of God as fire occurs several times in both the Old and the New Testaments. "Our God is a consuming fire," says the epistle to the Hebrews (12:29). But the fire here in Malachi is destructive only of what is base and worthless. It is a purifying, refining fire. And those who are being refined and purified are of value in God's sight, like gold and silver. The Levites who were responsible for leading the people in their worship are specifically named, for, if worship is to be worthy, leaders as well as people need cleansing, painful though it may be.

Yet this is essentially a message of hope. There is a future that will be better than the past, a future when offerings of priests and people will be acceptable to the Lord. Despite all the somber criticism of the book, Malachi is forward-looking, the past left behind, a future cleansed and renewed.

FOR MEDITATION

Search me, O God, and know my heart;
test me and know my thoughts.
See if there is any wicked way in me,
and lead me in the way everlasting.

PSALM 139:23–24

SOCIAL ILLS

To UNDERSTAND THESE verses, we need to realize that this chapter is not a simple sequence. The prophet's thought darts to and fro with the urgency of his solemn message. Verse 5 is not the sequel to the previous verse but reverts to the querulous question with which chapter 2 ended, "Where is the God of justice?" But justice also involves judgment (the Hebrew word *mishpat* carries both meanings), this time against all those among God's people who violate the integrity and destroy the liberty of others, whether by practicing magic and leading people away from God, or by adultery or oppression. All these diverse infringements of the liberties and rights of others stem from one underlying cause: " 'They do not fear me,' says the Lord of hosts" (v. 5). Malachi's social concern is beyond question. For him, worship and ethics coincide.

Many times over the centuries Israel's prophets had emphasized that our relationship to God and our treatment of our fellow humans are inseparable. Worship is unacceptable to God where there is no justice or compassion. The scribe who came to Jesus with the question, "Which commandment is the first of all?" understood this when he reaffirmed Jesus' words that love for God and love for our neighbor belong together, and added, "This is much more important than all whole burnt offerings and sacrifices." And Jesus replied, "You are not far from the kingdom of God" (Mark 12:32–34).

The Unchanging God

A NEW SECTION begins in verse 6 (as in NIV and REB) with God's affirmation that he is forever unchanging, despite the unfaithfulness and shifting loyalties of his people and the complaints of sceptics. Because God is dependable and reliable, there is still hope for the nation. The break in the relationship is not on his side. "Return . . ." he says, "and I will return to you" (v. 7). Although the restoration of the covenant relationship depends, as Malachi sees it, on the nation's willingness to take the first step (rather like the Gospel story of the prodigal son, who sets out for home of his own accord), yet the initiative that makes it possible is God's. Despite all the ills of the past, the unworthy worship, the social tensions that disrupted society and cast some into poverty while others grew rich, God offers a restoration of the relationship, an openhanded offer ready to respond generously to the nation's penitence.

But then comes another complaining question from the people. It is all very well to talk of returning to the Lord, but how are we to set about it? The answer comes in the following verses. Repentance requires action; it means open and generous giving. Of that, more in our next section.

A CHALLENGE AND PRAYER
Read 1 John 4:19–21:

We love because God first loved us. If someone says he loves God but hates his brother or sister, he is a liar. For he cannot love God, whom he has not seen, if he does not love his brother or sister, whom he has seen. The command that Christ has given us is this: Whoever loves God must love his brother also.

Lord, pour your love into our hearts, we pray, that it may overflow in blessing to those around us.

GOD'S GENEROUS OFFER

QUESTION FOLLOWS QUESTION. "How are we to return/repent?" say the people. God exposes the absurdity of the situation with a rhetorical question, "Will anyone rob God? Yet you are robbing me!" (v. 8) Jesus sometimes used a similar approach. Faced with a question by his opponents, he exposed the duplicity of their questioning and their attempts to entrap him by posing a question that demanded openness and honesty rather than clever arguments.

Malachi's contemporaries are perplexed by the blunt accusation; "How are we robbing you?" they ask. They are ignorant of God's requirements and of the nature of the God whom they profess to worship, so little have the priests fulfilled their role as teachers of God's law.

Yet, as always, God provides a way forward. Verses 10–12 are both a challenge and a promise. Malachi is often criticized for what may seem a mechanical, simplistic view of blessing. But such is unlikely. His intention throughout has been to expose the attitude that devalues commitment, chooses an easy way, and expects God's automatic response to purely external rituals. Malachi's expectation of God's imminent coming to purify both temple and worshipers (3:1–2) is counterbalanced here by the demand for practical action on the part of the people. The tithes were necessary to provide support for the Levites, who possessed no income of their own. How essential this was can be seen from the account of Nehemiah's time when the nonpayment of tithes resulted in the return of the Levites and singers, responsible for the temple services, to agricultural work in order to seek a livelihood which the offerings of the people should have provided (Nehemiah 13:10–11). Inevitably the temple was neglected and regular worship came to an end.

Wholehearted Response

"BRING THE FULL tithe into the storehouse," says the Lord through Malachi (v. 10). Here is the challenge to generous commitment to a generous

God. But God is no one's debtor, and the blessing he pours out will far exceed the gifts of the worshipers. There is nothing automatic about this, no diminution of God's sovereign freedom, but it is his promise of blessing that will result from wholehearted commitment. Then at last the community itself will be a delight to the Lord in whom they had professed to *delight* (3:1).

This joyful picture of overflowing blessing, however, is terminated abruptly at verse 13. Those who try to serve God faithfully are confronted by problems. It is not they, but the arrogant who seem to find happiness. Of what benefit are obedience and repentance? Worse still, those who do evil come off unscathed when they challenge God. In verse 10 they were invited to put God to the test to prove he keeps his promise. But here the test is different and so is its motivation. Its purpose is to prove God's indifference to human actions, his apathy with regard to human behavior.

It is sometimes supposed that belief in God was easier in prescientific days than it is in modern times. The evidence of Malachi disproves this. There were others, too, in earlier centuries who denied God's involvement in the world and deliberately overthrew the moral law (Isaiah 5:19–23). There were atheists, too, in the ancient world.

PRAYER
Lord, help us to commit ourselves unreservedly to you and to know in experience the fullness of your blessing.

THE LISTENING GOD

VERSES 13–15 HAVE been something of an aside after the promises of verses 10–12. Now, in response to the expectation of blessing, other voices speak. They are those of faithful worshipers who revere the Lord. They are not isolated believers, but together they share their faith; they "spoke with one another." Despite all that the sceptics had maintained about God's indifference to humanity, Malachi simply says, "The Lord took note and listened." And more than that, in the style of an eastern monarch (he is, after all, "a great king") God has a book of remembrance written, a permanent record of their commitment. Just such a book of remembrance is what King Ahasuerus had, in the story of Esther, in which her uncle Mordecai's action that had saved the king's life was recorded, a record that eventually saved Mordecai's own life and defeated the machinations of his enemy Haman (see Esther 6:1–2). The words of verse 17 are simple yet astounding. Here is the Lord, placing such value on those who revere him that he lays claim to them for himself: "They shall be mine . . . my special possession *(segullah)* on the day when I act."

Segullah is an interesting word. It is used of David's own personal treasures that he gave as an offering, a sign of his devotion to God (1 Chronicles 29:3). This special relationship, promised to Israel at the inauguration of the covenant made on Mount Sinai, does not detract from the fact that God is sovereign over all the earth. This is spelled out in Exodus 19:5–6: "If you obey my voice and keep my covenant, you shall be my treasured possession *(segullah)* out of all the peoples. Indeed, the whole earth is mine, but you shall be for me a priestly kingdom and a holy nation."

Here is the answer to the questions of the sceptics in verse 14. The difference between God's faithful servants and those who ignore his claims will be made plain on the coming day of the Lord. His advent, which brings blessing to some, will spell destruction for others. This is the only instance in Malachi where the terms "the righteous" and "the wicked" are used to denote two diametrically opposed groups. This was a time when moral distinctions had become blurred and when God's name was profaned in the very act of offering sacrifice (1:12). But Malachi's God is a just God to whom humans are accountable for their actions. His justice is tempered with mercy, as a father to his children, yet he is "the Lord of hosts," not a God who can be bent to human will.

With the language of the righteous and the wicked, we are once more in the realm of the psalms. In the prelude to the psalter the contrasting destinies of the righteous and the wicked are set out. The agricultural metaphors are striking:

> (The righteous) are like trees
> planted by streams of water,
> which yield their fruit in its season,
> and their leaves do not wither.
> In all that they do, they prosper.
> The wicked are not so,
> but are like chaff that the wind drives away.
>
> PSALM 1:3–4

PRAYER

Grant, Lord, that we may stand firm in the cause of truth and right, ever nourished by your word and strengthened by your Spirit.

A PROMISE OF HEALING

THE OPENING WORD immediately catches our attention: "See, the day is coming" (so the NRSV, representing the Hebrew "behold"). The prophet has no doubts about it. This is the day of joy and liberation for those who commit themselves to the Lord. The image of the sun with its healing rays, typifying the glory and saving power of God, is unique in the Old Testament. Israel had in general been wary of this kind of terminology, in contrast to the religions of Egypt and Mesopotamia, where the sun god was represented by a "winged" sun. In Psalm 84:11, however, the Lord is described simply as "a sun and a shield."

The destiny of each individual, whether of delight or of doom, depends upon personal and deliberate choice. God's offer of healing and liberation is open to all, but it requires the risk of faith, the kind of faith that is prepared for commitment to God, come what may. This is what is meant by revering his name (v. 2). The condemnation of arrogance that runs like a thread through much of the Old Testament is picked up here, singled out, for pride is the source of many sins. Wickedness is at last to be eliminated, root and branch. The emphasis here is not on vengeance but on the reversal of fortunes. Ashes were a common sign of mourning. Now those who caused that sorrow will be "ashes" under the feet of the liberated, not by evolution nor by revolution, but by divine intervention.

A Pointer to the Future

THE LAST THREE verses are widely recognized as a later addition, furnishing a conclusion not simply to Malachi but to the whole Book of the Twelve. The specific mention of Elijah fills out the vague reference to the Lord's messenger at the beginning of chapter 3. These two great figures, Moses and Elijah, traditionally represent the law and the prophets (hence their appearance with Jesus on the Mount of Transfiguration). It is appropriate that their names are linked together here at the end of Malachi since, in the Hebrew Bible, it forms the conclusion to the first two sections, the Law *(Torah)* and the prophets. The arrangement of the Christian Bible is different, and here Malachi is the conclusion to the whole of the Old Testament. It ends on a note that points forward to the New Testament. John the Baptist, the forerunner of the Messiah, proclaiming in the desert the way of the Lord, is compared by Jesus to Elijah. Malachi ends with the exhortation to remember the teaching of Moses. In the Sermon on the Mount, Jesus expounds Moses' teaching, giving to it a new and radical depth. The concept of sin deepens. Laws whose fulfillment was within human reach in the Old Testament become in the New Testament principles of such depth that they are beyond human keeping. Hence the gospel rests on God's grace, not on human righteousness.

REJOICE IN THE GOOD NEWS OF THE GOSPEL
In the apostle Paul's words:

No one is put right in God's sight by doing what the Law requires; what the Law does is to make man know that he has sinned. But now God's way of putting people right with himself has been revealed. It has nothing to do with law, even though the Law of Moses and the prophets gave their witness to it. God puts people right through their faith in Jesus Christ. God does this to all who believe in Christ.

ROMANS 3:20–22, GNB

NOTES

NOTES

NOTES

NOTES

NOTES

NOTES

NOTES